FIVE LOOKS AT ELIZABETH BISHOP

Titles by Anne Stevenson

ANNE STEVENSON

Five Looks at Elizabeth Bishop

BLOODAXE BOOKS

ISBN: 978 1 85224 725 6

This edition published 2006 by
Bloodaxe Books Ltd,
Eastburn,
South Park,
Hexham,
Northumberland NE46 1BS.

First published in hardback in 1998
by Bellew Publishing Company Ltd
in association with Agenda Editions.

www.bloodaxebooks.com
For further information about Bloodaxe titles
please visit our website and join our mailing list
or write to the above address for a catalogue.

Supported using public funding by

ARTS COUNCIL
ENGLAND

Cover design: Neil Astley & Pamela Robertson-Pearce.

This is a digital reprint of the 2006 Bloodaxe edition.

For Elizabeth Bishop's 'Dear Ilse'
and in memory of Kit Barker

Our visions coincided – 'visions' is
too serious a word – our looks, two looks:
art 'copying from life' and life itself,
life and the memory of it so compressed
they've turned into each other. Which is which?

'Poem'

Contents

Acknowledgements

The author's thanks must go first to her dedicatee, Ilse Barker (the writer, Kathrine Talbot) for advice, encouragement, editorial suggestions and innumerable re-readings. Warm thanks, too, to archivist Sandra L. Barry for her helpful letters and for material supplied in her book, *Elizabeth Bishop: An Archival Guide to Her Life in Nova Scotia*, and to Kathleen Carlton Johnson for sending me photocopies of articles and manuscripts from the Vassar College Library. Among many books indispensable to the writing of this introductory work I am indebted to *Elizabeth Bishop and Her Art*, edited by Lloyd Schwartz and Sybil P. Estess; David Kalstone's *Becoming a Poet*; Brett Millier's biography, *Elizabeth Bishop: Life and the Memory of It*; Gary Fountain and Peter Brazeau's *Remembering Elizabeth Bishop, An Oral Biography*; Victoria Harrison's *Elizabeth Bishop's Poetics of Intimacy* and Robert Giroux's beautifully edited *One Art: The Selected Letters of Elizabeth Bishop*. I am also grateful to Robert Giroux for granting me permission to quote from Elizabeth Bishop's writings and letters, and to Chatto & Windus for permission to quote from her books published in England.

Author's Preface

As many readers of Elizabeth Bishop will know, excellent introductions to her work already exist in David Kalstone's *Becoming a Poet* (1989) and Lloyd Schwartz and Sybil Estess's compendium, *Elizabeth Bishop and Her Art* (1983). So far in the 1990s, Victoria Harrison, Bonnie Costello and Lorrie Goldensohn in the United States have contributed thoughtful, scholarly studies to a galloping Bishop industry, while Seamus Heaney and James Fenton, in their lectures as Professors of Poetry at Oxford, have both singled out her work. In 1993, the publication of Brett Millier's detailed biography initiated what could be termed, I suppose, a stampede of Bishop-lovers to the Vassar archives. Millier's biography has meanwhile been amplified by an interesting (though rather less reliable) oral biography, *Remembering Elizabeth Bishop*, assembled by Gary Fountain and Peter Brazeau (1994), and by a hefty selection of the poet's letters edited by Robert Giroux and published in 1994 under the title *One Art*.

My reason for heaping yet another book about Bishop on the pile rests on a twofold indebtedness. More than any other contemporary, Elizabeth Bishop opened my eyes to possibilities and directions for poetry I might never have explored without her example. I have long wanted to thank her. More heavily on my conscience weighs the burden of having written, over thirty years ago, an introduction to her work that she liked at the time but later could not approve. In 1962, when as a graduate student at the University of Michigan I undertook to contribute a volume on Elizabeth Bishop to the Twayne United States Authors Series, so little material relating to her life and work was available that I was reduced to writing to Miss Bishop herself for guidance. At the time she was living in Brazil, and the letters she wrote back to me, warmly and exhaustively answering my questions, were so exciting and yet so far beyond anything I was in those days capable of assimilating, that I am today embarrassed by the sketch I offered to Twayne in 1965.

Fortunately, owing to a personal mishap, the letters Elizabeth Bishop addressed to me in connection with that Twayne volume found their way in the 1970s to the Special Collections Library of Washington University, St Louis. There, in the 1980s, Kalstone, Harrison and other scholars were able to consult them and put them to more pertinent use than I could possibly have done in the middle '60s. When I began my first book, Elizabeth Bishop had published only two collections, North & South and A Cold Spring; even when, in 1964, her New York agent sent me copies of the poems that later appeared in Questions of Travel, I was too young or too blindly intent on pursuing abstract ideas, to see how distinctly they marked a change of direction in her work.

Today, the ninety or so poems Elizabeth Bishop chose to publish in her lifetime – plus some, like 'Exchanging Hats', that she suppressed – are known to poetry readers throughout the English-speaking world. To some new readers, Bishop will be only a name. Others may have been taught to see her as a feminist or even lesbian poet. My object has been to suggest ways of reading Bishop uncategorically in the light of her insistence on looking at the world and finding there solid correlatives for the marvels, griefs and contradictions that shaped her personal geography. In order to focus my study on the continuities that over the years transfigured Bishop's art, I have limited my discussion to her principal stories, essays and poems. Though she was a fine translator from French, Portuguese and Spanish, I have not tried to explain why. And though she published amusing (rather trenchant) verse tributes to Marianne Moore and Ezra Pound, I have not seen that attempting to analyse them or other translucent lyrics could serve any useful purpose. Elizabeth Bishop herself was opposed to over-analysis. 'After a session with a few of the highbrow magazines one doesn't want to look at a poem for weeks,' she wrote, brusquely dismissing an authors' questionnaire in 1950.[1]

More questionable may be my omission of a chapter on Elizabeth Bishop's love poems. She did not write many, and she only published, to my knowledge, seven: 'Insomnia', the sequence of 'Four Poems' towards the end of *A Cold Spring*, followed by 'Argument' and her wonderful 'The Shampoo'. Of the Four Poems, 'O Breath' seems to me exceptionally fine. Spoken by an asthmatic, it uses spaces within the lines like broken breathing to indicate difficulties of communication between lovers. In recent years, two or three unpublished love poems to women by Elizabeth Bishop have been discovered among her papers, and of course much has been made of them by feminist scholars. My own gut feeling is that Bishop would not have wanted to expose these private poems to the public (she would have condemned them as art, in any case), and since there are so many poems more central to her work that yield up, after a little study, a sense of her truly genderless depth of understanding, it seemed unnecessary and perhaps voyeuristic to devote a chapter exclusively to her sexuality.

With so many books on Elizabeth Bishop crowding the libraries, anyone setting out to write something new has either to read them all with a view to agreement or refutation (that I have not done; it would have meant a very long book), or else rely on sources of information and leave critical discourse alone. My instinct was to read carefully through *The Complete Poems* and the *Collected Prose* before I looked at a single secondary work – though I confess I had already read David Kalstone's classic, *Becoming a Poet*, as I had Brett Millier's biography and Victoria Harrison's *Poetics of Intimacy*. These were books, together with *One Art* and my own correspondence with Bishop, that I continued to consult as I wrote, though my interpretations of individual poems are always my own.

The chronology at the end is also based on a first hand reading of Bishop, particularly of her published letters. It corrects mistakes, mostly regarding dates, that Bishop herself made when she sent me biographical information in the 1960s. In Britain, *The Complete Poems*, edited by Robert Giroux and published by Chatto & Windus in 1991, and the *Collected Prose*, also edited by Giroux and published by Chatto & Windus in 1994, remain in print. Thanks to the generosity of Bishop's publishers, I have not been restricted in my use of quotations, but I have assumed that readers who are interested enough in this exceptional American to read a book *about* her will also want to keep these collections close at hand.

ANNE STEVENSON
Pwllymarch, Llanbedr, Gwynedd
June, 1997

CHAPTER ONE

In the Waiting Room

But I felt: you are an *I*,
you are an *Elizabeth*,
you are one of *them*.
Why should you be one, too?

'In the Waiting Room'

Although I think I have a prize 'unhappy childhood,'
almost good enough for the text-books – please don't
think I dote on it.

Elizabeth Bishop, letter of 23 March 1964

'American poets are strange,' Donald Hall says bluntly in his
introduction to the 1969 Faber anthology, *American Poetry*, citing
Walt Whitman, Edgar Allan Poe, Emily Dickinson, and Hart Crane
as examples of suspiciously gifted New World oddballs. He could
have added Elizabeth Bishop to his list, although this poet's
strangeness took the form of a stubborn predisposition to be (not
just appear) as unstrange and inconspicuous as possible. Writing
in the *New York Review of Books* two months after Bishop's death,
James Merrill famously remarked on her 'instinctive, modest, life-
long impersonation of an ordinary woman.' Do I see Elizabeth
Bishop raising her eyebrows? 'Impersonation' suggests disguise or
pretence, and Bishop took a certain pride in being a bad pretender.
Any reading that traces the line of her development from baroque

imitation in her college years through a period of quasi-surrealism in the 1930s to the natural purity and depths of her autobiographical work must conclude that a part of her really *did* aspire to be unexceptional – not a lonely, looked-up-to poet and outsider, but a beloved, humanly accepted Elizabeth, if not one of them, most certainly one of us.

Mary McCarthy, interviewed in 1985, confirmed the plainness of Bishop's appeal with this example of her 'strangeness' in the world of New York intellectuals. Sometime in the summer of 1957, McCarthy took Elizabeth Bishop around to Hannah Arendt's apartment in the city. After formal introductions were completed, the assembled guests began discussing the interpretation of a certain line of verse, developing more and more abstruse ideas about its meaning. Elizabeth Bishop was the last to speak. 'Well,' she said, 'I would think that it was literally true.' She was convinced, says McCarthy, that 'anything in a poem was true, that it was there because it had happened.'[1] In the heyday of the New Criticism this would have been a novel, not to say heretical point of view, yet it was one Bishop held long before 'confessional poetry' made literal truth respectable in twentieth-century verse.

Bishop's view that poems can and should tell the truth represented the positive side of a scathing contempt for affected or pretentious art. She mostly preferred 'small-scale' works to 'grand all out efforts', and for an artist to lack interest in observation was, in her opinion, a cardinal sin. To write the 'truth' meant, for Bishop, first to *notice* all the aspects of something as it really happened, and then to set these down in a form that would delight, stimulate and amplify the understanding of other people who 'noticed'. You could say that being ordinary for Elizabeth Bishop was a way of choosing to be élitist. She was an observer who wrote for observers; an individual who spoke to individuals. She had little time for academic generalization and disliked critical theory. She attracted a devoted band of followers by making something of a fetish of her private tastes, but she also could be witty at the expense of these tastes. Shy with strangers, she was a good hater of everything cruel, fake, dull, insensitive, ugly, bad-mannered and commercially greedy. She took little interest in politics, but was innately conservative and, by her own admission, snobbish when it came to selecting friends. At the same time, as many of her poems demonstrate, she always felt profound sympathy for the poor. She was an authority on modern painting and baroque music, yet a lover of Baptist hymns, black spirituals, jazz, blues, and Brazilian sambas. As a personal correspondent, she was one of the most delightful letter-writers who ever lived.

No introductory portrait of Elizabeth Bishop would be complete, however, without acknowledging the cross-currents that throughout her life undermined her determination to live honestly and write well. A poem she wrote in 1979 – one of her very last – is the short-lined 'Sonnet' that begins 'Caught – the bubble/ in the spirit-level, / a creature divided.' Bishop herself was this divided creature, and it was to her own 'spirit-level' that her metaphor referred. The divisions that tore at Elizabeth Bishop were multiple, but most of them can be traced back to the bleak uncertainties – and some certainties, too – of her early childhood. This is why, although she did not find her way back to childhood until middle-aged and living in Brazil, it seems appropriate to begin by looking carefully at what she saw when she set her memories free.

Readers who have heard of Elizabeth Bishop but are unfamiliar with her poetry might do worse than approach her through her prose. Her instinct in fiction, as in poetry, was always to tell the truth, but while the truths that animate her early verse can seem dream-like or obscure, everything she wrote about her childhood is pellucid. The theme common to all Bishop's autobiographical stories is how a small child learns to overcome anxiety about happenings in the adult world by intently concentrating on *things*. Much of Elizabeth Bishop's writing is a poetry of *things* exalted or transmuted into a state of near spirituality – though her import is never religious as we usually understand the word. Shortly after she had met Marianne Moore in the spring of 1934, she mused in her notebook:

> It's a question of using the poet's proper material . . . i.e., immediate intense physical reactions, a sense of metaphor and decoration in everything – to express something not of them, something I suppose, spiritual. But it proceeds from the material, the material eaten out with acid, pulled down from underneath, made to perform and always kept in order, in its place . . . [2]

In *Becoming a Poet*, David Kalstone noted that much of Bishop's early writing divides the perceived world in two: on the one hand, a daylight place of delectable 'things' and adventures, on the other, a fearful, chaotic land of dreams and madness. In reconstructing her childhood, day-by-day and sometimes hour-by-hour, Bishop was empowered to bridge the gap between the world's outward delights and its hidden nightmares. More than this, by recreating from a safe distance the exact sensations of her small self, she could resume the survival technique that had taught her, probably before the age of five, to identify 'good' signs (or nameable things) in a world that was shadowy with unnamed 'bad' ones. This little girl is to be found at her most likeable in the autobiographical stories at the end of the *Collected Prose*: 'Gwendolyn', 'Memories of Uncle Neddy' and 'In the Village', as also in 'Primer Class' and 'The Country Mouse' at the beginning.

*　　*　　*

Elizabeth Bishop was born in Worcester, Massachusetts to a well-to-do father, who died when she was eight months old, and a young Nova-Scotian mother who never recovered from her husband's premature death. Elizabeth retained no memory of her father and seems not to have been affected by his loss. In 'The Country

Mouse' she lightly refers to the personal interpretation she used to give the lines 'Land where my father died / Land of the pilgrim's pride' when she sang them in her Massachusetts primary school. Her feelings about her mother, on the other hand, were complicated: a deadly mixture, so far as one can see, of longing, fear, resentment, guilt and, of course, pity.

After her husband died, aged thirty-nine, Gertrude Bulmer Bishop suffered acutely from what could have been manic depression or hyperthyroidism or both. Her melancholia eventually developed into a violent psychosis, for which, early in 1914, she was treated in a private clinic in Norwood, Massachusetts. In May 1915, when she seemed better, she returned with little Elizabeth to her parents in Great Village. Then, apparently in November 1915 and again in May 1916, she went back to Boston, without Elizabeth, perhaps for surgery. There is no record of Gertrude's attending the Norwood Clinic a second time, nor does evidence exist to support Bishop's own belief that her mother entered McLean's Sanatorium in Belmont. She did, however, receive treatment at Deaconness Hospital, Boston, though the hospital has no record of it; so it is not impossible that she was treated elsewhere, too.[3]

Wherever she went, Gertrude Bishop did not respond to the cures attempted. In June 1916, accompanied by her sister Grace, she came back home to Nova Scotia and almost immediately became permanently psychotic. Elizabeth was then five years old. The events related in Bishop's story 'In the Village' are all true, though it is not generally known that Gertrude herself accepted that she needed hospitalisation and agreed to enter the Dartmouth Sanatorium, near Halifax. She lived there until her death in May 1934, but her daughter never saw her again.

The Bulmer family did all they could for Gertrude. Fifty years later, Bishop was sure that her mother had received the best treatment available at the time. Certainly in Great Village every effort was made to make the virtually orphaned little girl feel at home. Photographs of Elizabeth Bishop at five or six show a happy-looking, round-faced child with shining eyes. Nowhere in her adult memoirs does she let fall the slightest hint of ill-usage or wilful unkindness on the part of her relatives. Devoted especially to her maternal grandparents and her aunt Grace, Elizabeth readily absorbed the Bulmers' undemonstrative affection, together with their puritanism and their Canadian black-tea-and-porridge dependability. The Bulmers themselves, however, could not have concealed their distress from their hypersensitive, watchful little granddaughter. Nor at a time when insanity was felt to be a family stigma could they pretend not to feel guilt and shame. The worst of it, Elizabeth told me in 1964, was that by returning to Nova Scotia before her final breakdown, Gertrude had forfeited her chances of more up-to-date treatment in Boston: she had lost her American citizenship when her husband died, and the immigration authorities refused to allow her back, sick, into the United States.[4]

Towards the end of 'In the Village' – a story told entirely from the child's point of view – the sorrowing grandmother is shown packing weekly parcels of cake and sweetmeats to send to her daughter in the Dartmouth sanatorium. The child hastens through the village to the post office with one of these packets, hiding the address from anyone she might meet on the way. 'The address of the sanatorium,' she tells us, 'is in my grandmother's hand-writing, in purple indelible pencil . . . It will never come off.' In the single word 'indelible' every incident associated with Gertrude Bishop's breakdown, like the parcel itself, is carefully packed. We are told, first of all, that a scream or the echo of a scream hangs over the village, 'a slight stain in those pure blue skies . . . Flick the lightning rod on top of the church steeple with your fingernail and you will hear it.'

This is, of course, the mother's scream 'indelibly' heard by the real five-year-old Elizabeth on a hot day in June, 1916. The story shows the child as apprehensive of her mother, fearful that some terrible event will occur (has she heard the scream before?), although the climate of dread in which the first part of the story takes place is never explained. Instead, the fear is embodied in – and deflected by – a number of desirable but sadly flawed objects: a set of glittering, disintegrating postcards; a beautiful set of china, pieces of which turn out to be broken when it is unpacked; the mother's mourning clothes that the child thinks are clothes to be worn in the morning. She hovers in the background, watching her mother being fitted for a purple dress – she has been persuaded 'to come out of mourning' – in the front bedroom. Miss Gurley, the dressmaker, crawls around 'eating pins as Nebuchadnezzar had crawled eating grass,' and it can be no accident that this fleeting reference to the mad, surely purple-clad, Biblical king immediately precedes the *clang* of the blacksmith's hammer outside.

Nate, shaping horseshoes in his dark, glistening forge next door, 'sweating hard' in a leather apron and bare chest, is already purging the village of 'wrongness' with his counter-music on the anvil. 'Clang! The pure note, pure and angelic.' The sound is soot-covered poetry, 'real' and physical, with a power to turn 'everything else to silence'; and it arrives just in time. For imme-diately following the blacksmith's *clang*, the mother decides that the dress is all wrong and screams. 'The child vanishes.' A few lines more, though, and the little girl shows up again under the lilacs and honeysuckle in the blacksmith's cave of making. Here, like the god Vulcan, Nate is hurling moon after 'bloody little moon' into a 'tub of night black water standing by the forge.' An attendant horse 'nods his head as if agreeing to a peace treaty.' And peace is indeed momentarily restored, though the mother and aunts soon appear, sitting on the back porch sipping 'raspberry vinegar' that should be sweet-tasting but obviously isn't.

Upon a warp and woof of contrasting sounds – the mother's destructive scream and the healing 'angelic' *clang* of the black-smith – Elizabeth Bishop has woven a classical allegory (however small-scale) of Good battling with and finally overcoming Evil. 'In the Village', however, is more than a moral parable. For its author it represented the culmination of who knows how many earlier, failed attempts to confront and recreate the scene of her mother's breakdown.[5]

*   *   *

Gertrude Bishop died in Dartmouth Hospital on May 29th, 1934, the year her daughter graduated from Vassar. In March of the same year, Elizabeth met and became a protegée of forty-seven-year-old Marianne Moore. Miss Moore and her mother lived together in their Brooklyn apartment (famously 260 Cumberland Street), and many a critic has since speculated about the effect the example of this mutually dependent mother and daughter had on the motherless Miss Bishop. Whatever the case, soon after leaving Vassar, Elizabeth sailed with a friend to Cuttyhunk island, off Cape Cod, and there started to write something her letters of the time refer to as 'my novel'. Calling it *The Proud Villagers*, she planned to build it around the 'dailiness' of Nova Scotia village life: the dour speech, 'harsh and inverted', the villagers' reluctance to show affection, her grandmother an exception to this rule, the household's 'heavy cooking and . . . black tea.' If Bishop got any further with her novel that summer, it has not survived.

Sometime the following winter, while living alone in New York, Bishop took up her theme again, creating a boy called Lucius De Brisay (after a family in Great Village) to stand in for her child-self, and probably sketching out a plot centered on the mental breakdown of his (her) mother, Easter. Again, no one knows how much Elizabeth Bishop wrote of this story or how much she threw away.

A more extensive series of notes survives, seemingly from the autumn of 1936 when the poet was once again living in New York after a year's travel in Europe. As Harrison comments, these later pages of narrative are quite unlike the surrealistic poetry and fables Bishop was mostly writing at the time.[6] It seems probable that Bishop's self-censoring guilt about her mother was being reinforced by the fierce aesthetic fastidiousness she admired in Marianne Moore. A good deal of the draft of 1936 has been slashed – especially sections which open for inspection the sealed closet of the Bulmer family's grief. Attempts to describe Easter and her childish behaviour, together with the adult pressure Lucius is made to feel (so much so that his sleep is troubled by St Vitus Dance) are savagely crossed out:

> In the night she [Easter] began to cry very gently and complain-ingly like a good child that's stood all it can. She made little imploring noises, asking someone for something/I sat up & pulled my boots on & took the stick from under the window & shut that, then I sat on the edge of the bed waiting for Aunt Grace. ~~She began to cry louder Suddenly~~ the door opened & Aunt Grace, holding the little lamp, stuck her head in and said very low: 'I guess you'll have to come Lucius.' ~~Maybe she wants you.~~' I took the lamp. We walked along the hall. Just as we got to the door Aunt Grace said, 'Oh ~~Lucius~~ – I don't know what to do – '[7]

After struggling through forty pages of this 1936 draft, Bishop apparently abandoned her novel altogether – though she kept her notes and scraps – until she began to think about Nova Scotia when she was living in Brazil, seventeen years later. Translating a Brazilian classic, *Minha Vida de Menina* (*The Diary of Helena Morley*) – the diary of a real little girl brought up in a remote diamond-mining village – Elizabeth was reminded strongly of her own childhood. But this time, in 1952, she knew how to go about retrieving her past. She would hold up her memory like a mirror to Great Village and distance the pain of her recollections by off-loading emotions onto places and people she could still see and hear. She had always collected precious things – pictures, books, toys, ornaments, shells and stones, junk-shop finds and unusual artifacts. These were *trouvées* she could describe exactly, so that each object would become a talisman, so to speak, of the painful occasion it stood for. Whether Bishop was conscious of a new empowerment or not (she may simply have discovered that the stories were ready to be 'born'), she wrote 'Gwendolyn' and 'In the Village' with comparative ease and was proud of the results.

These two stories, then, are all that remain of Bishop's long-projected novel, and they are masterpieces. In both, the child recalled is nameless, an 'I' (and of course, equally an 'eye') who remembers the events of her past in a vocabulary of settings, objects and animals. 'Gwendolyn' opens with a description of grown-up Aunt Mary's doll, produced by 'grandmother' from its tissue-paper wrappings for a child sick with bronchitis. We are not told why the grandmother is a grandmother and not a mother, but through the details of the doll's 'toy steamer trunk of green tin' and her 'exciting' skating costume with 'white glace-kid boots' on which are sewn 'a pair of too-small, dull-edged but very shiny skates', enough is said to establish a setting that is wonderful (full of wonders for the child) and at the same time ordinary and obscurely dangerous: the human setting, in short, of all Bishop's major writings.

The abundance of description in 'Gwendolyn' does not contribute much to its plot, but every detail helps verify the reality of a tale that in cruder hands might have become maudlin. Gwendolyn Appletree (in real life, Gwendolyn Patriquin) was the youngest child and only daughter – 'blond and pink and white' like sugar candy – in a large family of boys. The 'I' of the story, an eight- or nine-year-old Elizabeth, looks upon Gwendolyn as something untouchable, a creature quite as precious as Aunt Mary's treasured doll. Her grandparents, though, think Gwendolyn is spoiled, and Elizabeth uneasily senses their head-shaking disapproval when Gwendolyn's parents allow her to eat cake and ice-cream although they know she is likely to die of diabetes.

Several summer episodes – a church picnic, an afternoon's play – bring the two girls together. Then two days after Gwendolyn has spent the night at Elizabeth's house, she does die. When her funeral is held in the Presbyterian Church opposite the Bulmer farmhouse, Elizabeth, who is supposed not to know what is going on, observes with dreadful apprehension that her grandmother is crying. Half curious, half frightened, she steals into the forbidden front parlor and peeps through the lace curtains. Two men come into view carrying Gwendolyn's small white coffin which they set down on the grass by the church door before disappearing inside. Faced for a moment with the dead Gwendolyn, all alone, 'shut invisibly inside her coffin forever', the child at the window suddenly realizes what death means: not a pretty memorial stone with a lamb on it in the village cemetery, but a nothingness that lasts for ever and ever. In a single sentence the emotion that has so far been locked securely into cool description is released:

> Then I ran howling to the back door, out among the startled white hens, with my grandmother, still weeping, after me.

Even here, the 'startled white hens' anchor the unbearable in the ordinary. Immediately, though, Bishop shies away from this scene of anguish and devotes several sentences to finding some object that will absorb it. She comes up with a basket of marbles. They had been much treasured marbles when new, but somehow they had got pushed to the back of a cupboard, and when she remembered where they were and retrieved them, they were dismally covered with grime and dust. One marble in particular she had cherished – a big pink one that had 'moved me almost to tears to look at.' Finding this beautiful object 'dead' had given her a 'terrifying thrust', exactly the thrust she had felt seeing Gwendolyn's coffin lying alone by the church door. Of course, when her grandmother washed the pink marble it had come out looking good as new. Perhaps some such act of renewal could also be performed for Gwendolyn? And indeed, at the end of the story, we are shown how – in performance, in art – it is.

The final episode centres once more on Aunt Mary's doll. A month or so after the funeral, Elizabeth's grandparents go away for the day, leaving her with her aunt and small cousin Billy. The children are supposed to be playing in Billy's yard, but instead they sneak back to their grandparents' where Elizabeth does something 'very bad'. She fetches down the forbidden doll from its drawer to show to her cousin. The children consider playing 'operation' on the doll's stomach ('we were rather too much in awe of her for that') but eventually they light upon the idea of adorning her with flowers and giving her a funeral. The doll importantly becomes for them a resurrected Gwendolyn, and the make-believe funeral – for which the children are punished – knits together all the threads of her sad little story in a ceremony that is 'perfectly beautiful'.

Parallels between 'Gwendolyn' and 'In the Village' are everywhere to be found: overpowering emotion in both stories is deflected into events or objects; the unbearable is borne and then absorbed into daily life. Tragedy occurs, but triumph ensues – untriumphantly, naturally, in the course of time. *Clang!* goes the blacksmith's hammer in the final paragraphs of 'In the Village'; *slp* says the river. 'Wild with joy,' the children at the end of 'Gwendolyn' realize that the doll's funeral has 'saved' her.

Bishop never stooped to be less than just to her autobiographical material, but her memoirs, as distinct from those two true stories, have more of tolerant humour about them and less of tragedy. 'Primer Class' and 'Memories of Uncle Neddy' – both set in Great Village – could be described as delightful; as can even 'The Country Mouse', with its true-to-life account of how the Bishop grandparents altruistically 'kidnapped' their granddaughter from Great Village in the naïve belief that they could make a young lady of her in the gloomy magnificence of their house in Worcester.

Other fictions set in Nova Scotia are not quite so satisfying. Although an early published story 'The Baptism' found its way to the honour roll of *The Best Short Stories of 1938*, its stark, evangelical plot and fanatical main character owe too much, perhaps, to Southern realists like Carson McCullers and Eudora Welty. The same must be said of 'The Farmer's Children', a tale Bishop herself condemned as 'very bad' (see Giroux's introduction to Bishop's *Collected Prose*, xxi). By normal standards these fictions were, of course, pretty good. Any writer other than Elizabeth Bishop would have happily gone on to become a creditable American short-story writer. That Bishop never attempted anything like literary naturalism again must be put down to her extreme fastidiousness – and perhaps not unimportantly to a strong feeling that she ought be writing something else. Like a diamond, Bishop's talent was not easy to cut. The lucid accessibility that distinguishes her prose was hard won. So was the much considered but simple language of the autobiographical poems she wrote around the same time, in the 1950s and early '60s.

*   *   *

By the time Bishop had settled in Brazil, Marianne Moore – though still an honoured friend – was no longer her aesthetic sounding-board. Instead, Robert Lowell, seven years younger than Bishop but already more celebrated, was pressing her through his own example to find poems in her personal past. The American edition of Bishop's 1965 collection, *Questions of Travel*, sandwiches 'In the Village' between two sections of verse, the first called 'Brazil', the second, 'Elsewhere'. 'Elsewhere', as one might expect, meant chiefly Great Village, where the ballad-like 'Manners: for a child of 1918', 'Sestina', 'First Death in Nova Scotia' and probably 'Filling Station' (the latter not so personal) are set.

Readers of Bishop's Nova Scotia stories will find the cast of the first three poems familiar. The same grandfather, shorn of his gruffness, serves as an example of thoughtfulness to humans and animals in the light-hearted, anti-progressive 'Manners'. In 'Sestina', the child of 'In the Village' and 'Gwendolyn' reappears in the company of the same tearful grandmother, the latter rather more poignantly realized than before. In a famous essay, 'Domestication, Domesticity, and the Otherworldly', Helen Vendler drew attention to the 'domestic focus, of all six of 'Sestina's 's line-endings save one, 'tears'.[8] House, grandmother, child, stove, almanac are all homely words, indicative of safety; yet 'tears' manipulates the poem, undermining its comforts and revealing in its irregular four-stress lines a fearful gulf that divides what should be from what is:

> September rain falls on the house.
> In the failing light, the old grandmother
> sits in the kitchen with the child
> beside the Little Marvel Stove,
> reading the jokes from the almanac,
> laughing and talking to hide her tears.

'Little Marvel Stove' is a trade name that doubles as a pun; for though it can produce marvels – water from the teakettle 'dancing like mad on the hot black stove' – the drops this evening are like tears. The rain, too, is tears; and the grandmother's teacup is full of 'dark brown tears' that the child's drawing can do nothing to remedy. Even the man she puts into her picture has buttons like tears. The poem is arranged around end-words repeated in the strict order of the sestina-form, producing a sombre effect without having to identify its cause. If we know the truth about Elizabeth Bishop's mother, we can fill the sorrowing gap with her name that 'Sestina' leaves unmentioned. If we don't, the poem is perhaps even more powerful. Unspecified, its grief becomes universal and inevitable:

> It was to be, says the Marvel Stove.
> I know what I know, says the almanac.

What at first seems most appealing about 'Sestina' is its stoic matter-of-factness. The grandmother naively believes that personal disasters are fated to happen; the almanac knows what it knows. Yet the poem's fatalistic message – if that's what it is – is contradicted at the end by a marvel after all. In the final stanzas, the 'little moons' on the pages of the almanac 'secretly' fall down like tears into the flower bed the child has drawn around her house:

Time to plant tears, says the almanac.
The grandmother sings to the marvellous stove
and the child draws another inscrutable house.

These three final lines suggest nothing so much as that the child, ordered by the almanac to plant the moon-like tears (of imagination?) has already begun to embed them in art. While the grandmother finds solace in singing (no doubt hymns) to the 'marvellous stove', the child is mysteriously at work on 'another inscrutable house' that is *not* foretold by the almanac. Instead, it is (or will be) created by herself from the planted tears. Each tear, when it grows and flowers in the future, will release the very images of house, grandmother, child, stove, almanac and tears out of which she, the poet, has built her sestina.

That the artist in his or her freedom is called upon to transform the terrible into the marvellous is a theme that runs right though Bishop's writing – as, for example, in 'The Weed' in which drops of river-water carry into the future all the scenes they have ever reflected. 'Belief' is too crude a word to describe this poet's tentative faith in the miraculous. By calling attention to a continuous, enduring life that is extraneous to human concerns, she raises domestic events in 'Sestina' and 'In the Village' to a level that must be called spiritual. In Bishop's own words, she lays down 'material' that when 'eaten out with acid' or 'pulled down from underneath' produces 'something not of them' but which nonetheless seems 'enormously important.'9

It is worth pointing out that while 'Gwendolyn' and 'In the Village' summon a wealth of detail to reflect or stand in for the narrator's emotions, 'Sestina' triumphs mainly because of its fugue-like form. Almost certainly, the poet brought her mind to bear on her material first, and then found a form not to *fit* it but *to pull up from beneath* its spiritual import. In this respect, the more a poem deliberately structures its material, the more surprised the poet is likely to be to find herself unearthing something important she didn't expect. In an illuminating essay, the American poet Chase Twichell argues that in Bishop's work 'it's not that the emotion is camouflaged or unacknowledged; rather, it's written around as though it were each poem's [unspoken] center of gravity. Each poem has a hole at its heart, a hollow spot.'[10] Twichell's insight helps to explain the unusual power of Bishop's seemingly flat language in 'Sestina' and in the poem that follows it, 'First Death in Nova Scotia'.

'First Death in Nova Scotia' is drawn from the autobiographical material recounted in 'Memories of Uncle Neddy'*; 'Little cousin Arthur' laid out in the 'cold, cold parlor' was a younger brother of Billy in 'Gwendolyn'. Sandra Barry tells me that this baby, whose real name was Frank, was only two months old when he died. The gravitational 'hollow spot' in the poem (set somewhat earlier than the Great Village stories) is not this time the speaker's mother, who, for once, is present. It's more that, as in 'Gwendolyn', the language circles round the fact of death itself. Although apparently written in free verse, the poem is tightly structured, with three heavy stresses per line (to slow the rhythm to the pace of a dirge), ten lines per stanza, and the whole threaded together with irregular rhymes.

Once more, the speaker is the child, Elizabeth, who takes comfort at first from some reassuring chromographs of the royal family she observes on the wall. Her attention, however, is soon drawn to a stuffed loon uncle Arthur* once 'fired a bullet into.' Since then 'it hadn't said a word.' This loon who keeps so mum about its death-experience is significantly attractive – beautiful, 'caressable' with 'desirable' red glass eyes. As the child – obviously the same little girl who coveted shiny marbles and glittering postcards in the stories – is given a white lily and lifted up to say 'goodbye' to her baby cousin, the sudden action shatters the frozen tableau. For the first time, the dead child is observed realistically by the living one:

* In life, Bishop's uncle Arthur.

Arthur was very small.
He was all white, like a doll
that hasn't been painted yet.
Jack Frost had started to paint him
the way he always painted
the Maple Leaf (Forever).
He had just begun on his hair,
a few red strokes, and then
Jack Frost had dropped the brush
and left him white, forever.

Unlike 'Gwendolyn', 'First Death in Nova Scotia' refuses to end
on an upbeat – although the pun in 'Maple Leaf (Forever)' and the
homely touch given to Jack Frost and later to the 'gracious royal
couple' with their feet 'well wrapped up' may provoke adult
smiles. Just the same, at the end there is no hint that the child is
satisfied with Arthur's future:

They [the royal couple] invited Arthur to be
The smallest page at court.
But how could Arthur go,
clutching his tiny lily,
with his eyes shut up so tight
and the roads deep in snow?

* * *

For her third collection, *Questions of Travel* (1965), Elizabeth
Bishop completed only three family poems set in the recollected
Nova Scotia of her childhood. ('Large Bad Picture' in her first
book, was written in 1944, in Key West.) Notes and drafts over the
years show that she attempted several more: an elegy for her Aunt
Maud Shepherdson, who died in 1940; and then a second poem
focusing on domestic life in the Shepherdson's Boston tenement.
Remembering a phrase of her grandmother Bulmer's – 'nobody

knows' – Bishop considered a lightish poem about all 'three' of her grandmothers (one of them a great-grandmother) each of whom repeated a characteristic refrain. One stanza would be based on that familiar 'nobody knows'; another, on her Grandmother Bishop's more ominous 'My day will come', and a third on great-grandmother Hutchinson's 'Ho-hum. Ho-hum, hum a-day.'

After considering in turn the resigned iterations of these 'three average Christian ladies of their day', she would conclude by wondering 'What dismal phrase will come to me?'.[11] However amusing such an exercise might have become, Bishop got almost nowhere with it.

She also tried and failed – over a period of thirty or more years – to write a poem, or sometimes a story, about her young mother's school-teaching days in Cape Breton. To be titled 'Homesickness', it would recount the family legend of how the inexperienced sixteen-year-old had been expected to teach pupils who spoke nothing but Gaelic, and how, when she grew lonely, the family dog had been brought up to keep her company. Drafts of this story/ poem – with others about her mother's clothes or how her mother's fingers were bitten by a swan during a swanboat ride in Boston – survive only in strangled phrases, suggesting that the closer Bishop came to the reality of her mother, the less capable she was of transmuting life into art.

Much later, in the 1970s, Bishop got quite a way with a poem addressed to her grandfather Bulmer. Unlike 'First Death in Nova Scotia', its setting is dream-like, almost nightmarish as she pursues his home-like figure through eternal Nova Scotian snows. Four drafts exist, the last of which ends:

> If I should overtake you, kiss your cheek,
> its silver stubble would feel like hoar-frost
> and your old-fashioned, walrus moustaches
> be hung with icicles.

Creak, creak . . . frozen thongs and creaking snow.
These drifts are endless I think; as far as the Pole
They hold no shadows but their own, and ours.
Grandfather please stop! I haven't been this cold
                                        in years.[12]

The juxtapostion in this draft of 'the domestic and the strange' never, as Bishop realized, freed itself enough from the range of the personal to become universal. (Compare it, for instance, to the grandparents evoked in 'The Moose'.) It is typical, nevertheless, of how Bishop tried to make real people participate in an imaginary, domesticated eternity. I shall want to explore this time-theme further, but for now, we might look at the last poem Bishop completed for which she took material straight out of childhood experience. It is called 'In the Waiting Room', the first of ten poems in her last collection, *Geography III* (1976).

The structure of 'In the Waiting Room' resembles that of 'First Death in Nova Scotia': short two- or three-stressed lines are casually counterpointed against a prose-like narrative. If anything, the tone is even more colloquial and relaxed than in the earlier poem. This time, the setting is Worcester, Massachusetts, during the eight months or so when Elizabeth lived with her Bishop grandparents and her grown-up Uncle John and Aunt Florence. (See her memoir, 'The Country Mouse'.) We are even told the date of Aunt Consuelo's visit to the dentist: 'the fifth of February, 1918', three days before Elizabeth's seventh birthday.

Such an exact fixing of the day, with its grown-up people sitting in the dentist's waiting room and its 'horrifying' photographs in *The National Geographic*, is again typical of the way Bishop adopted a prosy, laid-back tone when she intended to sneak up on a serious question. 'In the Waiting Room' is, in fact, a poem about existential terror. The child, Elizabeth, surrounded by ordinary Americans, sits scrutinizing exotic scenes in the magazine, when without warning she is hurled into a dangerous, inhospitable universe.

When from inside the dentist's office her aunt's voice utters 'an oh! of pain', the child discovers that the cry is hers, too: 'my voice, in my mouth':

> Without thinking at all
> I was my foolish aunt,
> I – we – were falling, falling,
> our eyes glued to the cover
> of the *National Geographic,*
> February, 1918.

You can see why it was important to anchor such a shock in a date and a place. Not only do the child and her aunt share a family voice, they share human destiny. The terrifying significance of the revelation is that the child discovers *herself* in the same instant that she learns she is not unique. She is like everybody else: 'you are an I,/ you are an Elizabeth,/ you are one of them.'

It is this *double realization* of her own identity within the vastness and variability of the species that threatens to topple the child off 'the round turning world / into cold, blueblack space.' Without *The National Geographic* of February 1918 to hang on to, and without reminding herself that in three days she will be seven years old, Bishop would not convince us – as I think she does – that ordinary life is the most astonishing and terrible thing there is. Why should she be herself? And why, too, was she doomed to be one of *them* – one of the dull, unappealing people in the waiting room and somehow at the same time, one of those black naked women with 'horrifying' breasts in *The National Geographic*? How could human beings be all one, and yet each be individual? And if this was really so, how well – 'unlikely':

> I knew that nothing stranger
> had ever happened, that nothing
> stranger could ever happen.

For the nearly-seven-year-old, experiencing this strangest of

strangenesses was even more overpowering than the doleful truth
that had struck her when she viewed Gwendolyn's coffin lying alone
on the grass. The revelation in the *waiting* room (waiting for what?
truth? adulthood? knowledge?) was more like a traumatic shattering
of childlike ignorance: awful, but at the same time, shocking enough
to force upon her a new idea of the world, to open a window onto
a wider, more puzzling existence. Like a miniature Saul on the road
to Damascus, she was struck, felled, and when she came to, she
knew instantly that for better or worse she was 'in for it'.

Since Bishop's waiting-room experience also concludes 'The
Country Mouse', we can pretty well take it for granted that 'it really
happened' – though in the prose memoir her 'feeling of absolute
and utter desolation' is unambiguous, and no play on the word
'waiting' gives it mysterious dimensions. We have Bishop's word
for it that the facts so carefully mustered for 'In the Waiting Room'
are not all accurate. In an interview with George Starbuck pub-
lished in *Ploughshares*, she confessed that her memory had
confused two different issues of the *National Geographic*: the
naked African women who so alarmed her had not appeared in the
February issue, but in the *next* issue, in March. Having sent the
poem to *The New Yorker*, she went to check her facts in New York
Public library and there discovered her mistake.[13]

Of course the poem suffers not at all from this minor lapse in
otherwise perfect recall. Its masterly execution – that controlled,
natural tone, without one hysterical phrase or unnecessary word –
depends not on whether the facts are exact but on how convincingly
they are deployed. What seems beyond doubt is that Elizabeth
Bishop was from childhood prone to suffer from shattering black-
outs. In notes jotted down in June 1935, aboard the (Nazi) ship
Königstein, on the way to Europe, she recorded being twice

> . . . overtaken by an awful awful feeling of deathly physical and
> mental illness . . . It is as if one were whirled off from all the
> world and the interests of the world in a sort of cloud – dark,

sulphurous gray – of melancholia. When this feeling comes I can't speak, swallow, scarcely breathe. I knew I had had it once before, years ago, and last night on its second occurrence I placed it as 'homesickness'. . .[14]

'In the Waiting Room' probably reaches back to that 'once before'; it describes, certainly, a deathly experience, but instead of melancholia, it records a sense of being knocked out of time, and then of being suddenly knocked back into it:

> The waiting room was bright
> and too hot. It was sliding
> beneath a big black wave,
> another, and another.
>
> Then I was back in it.
> The War was on. Outside,
> in Worcester, Massachusetts,
> were night and slush and cold,
> and it was still the fifth
> of February, 1918.

This shattering waiting-room 'vastation' – a word coined by the elder Henry James – took place in the unhappiest year of Elizabeth Bishop's childhood. Torn away from Great Village, she found her Bishop grandparents, however well-meaning, remote. Their large, clapboard farmhouse some way out from the center of Worcester felt spiritless and gloomy, and with her older 'foolish' aunt and 'teasing' uncle she had nothing in common. As she confides in 'The Country Mouse', the close companions of her loneliness were chiefly the bull-terrier, Beppo, and a Swedish maid. The school she attended was satisfactory until she developed appalling eczema in addition to her asthma. Once her eczema sores were so severe that she was sent home in what she interpreted as disgrace. Later she attributed her abnormal shyness to shame suffered at school; and it was followed by more sick, lonely months after she was taken to live with her aunt and uncle Shepherdson in Boston.

So the motherless isolation of Bishop's childhood scarred her for life. And yet the stories and poems she wrote about it – looking back – are so alive with detail and written in so spirited and amusing a style that it is hard to believe it was quite so bad as she sometimes claimed. In many ways, her peculiar childhood gave her advantages. Great Village, however primitive, sounds the ideal place for an imaginative little girl to grow up; indeed, Bishop's stories turn it into something of an idyll. In Worcester and Boston, true, she was sick and miserable. Nonetheless, her despised uncle Jack, noting her loneliness, sought out one of the best boarding schools in Massachusetts and saw to it that she went there. Without the academic discipline provided by Walnut Hill, she might never have gone to Vassar, and without Vassar, she might not have met Marianne Moore or come to know the friends who became lifelines to her in the years ahead. For a young poet, there were even compensations for being bedridden. By the time she entered college, Elizabeth had read most of the major English and American classics. She was older than her classmates, better-informed and much more independent-minded. There have been worse childhoods. Growing up among uncles, aunts and cousins was not the same, certainly, as growing up in what we oddly call a nuclear family. Elizabeth must have absorbed very early the notion that she was set apart, special, or at least different from other people. The horror of the waiting-room revelation was precisely the onset of an inkling that maybe she was not.

In another way, too, Elizabeth Bishop was privileged in her loneliness. From an early age she was financially independent. She never disposed of a lot of money (though some of her Vassar friends did), yet up until the 1970s, she lived comfortably enough on money she had inherited from her father. She was subsidized, too, by literary prizes and fellowships, so she never really *had* to support herself until inflation seriously reduced the value of her income. Such unusual freedom to travel, explore, form interesting relationships and write under no pressure other than her own ambition, in some respects worked to her advantage. In others, it did not. Independence made her imaginatively bold but socially insecure. As a young woman, she moved fearlessly into a world of fishing, sailing, painting and travelling, and she knew all the most distinguished poets of her day. Still, she found intimacy difficult; a melancholia she could not control periodically drove her to drink, and, in the shadow of her alcoholism, none of the relationships she formed with women lasted very long – until she went to live with Lota de Macedo Soares in Brazil.

From her writings we can deduce that the 'creature divided' in Elizabeth Bishop was created in childhood when she herself perceived that a social gulf separated her two families. The rural, comparatively poor Bulmers had almost nothing in common with the rich, more conventional Bishops, though the families, so far as we know, never quarrelled. On the contrary, they cooperated, both families seeming to understand that a girl as sensitive and sickly as Elizabeth needed special attention. As she grew up, however, Elizabeth's divided self seems to have fragmented further. The precocious girl suffered adult traumas, such as that in the waiting room, and therefore never quite dared to abandon the dependency of childhood. Sometime in her teens, she became aware that the outward world of nature with which she had long been happy to identify was a reality quite distinct from the nightmarish, creatively fertile world of her dreams. This 'split' became a major theme of her poems in the 1930s.

Again, when after years of loneliness in Boston she made friends at last at school and college, she adored some of her favourites with a passion she was ashamed to show. And since all these friends were women, such passions, as she knew, were 'wrong' in the eyes of the (then) conventional world. Any and all of these divisions within the 'I' that called herself Elizabeth Bishop could have been responsible for her alcoholism – which constituted yet another 'split' in her character, for Elizabeth Bishop drunk, as many of her friends have testified, became a distressing caricature of the charming, intelligent woman that was Elizabeth Bishop sober.

We know from her letters – especially those written to her New York doctor, Anny Baumann – how much Elizabeth Bishop suffered from a whole battery of 'splits', not least from a dangerous one that gaped between her idea of what she, as an artist, should be accomplishing and a counterproductive antiself full of doubts and illnesses nourished by her sense of guilt. It is all the more extraordinary, therefore, that her poems, when she worked on them long enough, almost always achieved a classical lucidity and detachment. In the light of her poetic intelligence – when she was empowered to summon it – Bishop's personal dilemmas grew smaller, more outward-looking, more accessible, and in the end, mysteriously acceptable. Her method, as we have seen, was almost never – save in a few love poems – to allow uncontrollable clouds of emotion to spoil the lucidity of her art, and almost never to let personal anguish deflect her eye from the material at hand. Look, for instance, at how she starts one of the 'big' poems in her second book, 'Over 2,000 Illustrations and a Complete Concordance' (*A Cold Spring*, 1955). Once again, we see that the way in leads through childhood.

The poem begins 'Thus should have been our travels:', and goes on to describe the engraved illustrations in a large family Bible (doubtless the Bulmers') all of which 'resolve themselves' into one satisfactory Christian belief. Those convincing 'lines the burin made', like 'God's spreading fingerprint', are points of rest and safety in comparison to the disparate, senseless scenes the poet remembers from her own travels: St John's in Newfoundland; St Peter's in Rome; Mexico where she saw a dead man; rotting hulks in Ireland; a genteel tea in England; brothels in Marrakesh; and most appalling of all, a supposedly holy 'paynim prophet's' grave full of dust. How were such sights to be explained without belief?

> Everything only connected by 'and' and 'and.'
> Open the book. (The gilt rubs off the edges
> of the pages and pollinates the fingertips.)
> Open the heavy book.

That pollinating 'gilt' can be read, too, as 'guilt', suggesting that the poet, no longer a Christian, has lost her childhood faith but has found nothing to put in its place. Disillusion threatens to end the poem in nihilism, but instead Bishop, with passionate nostalgia, turns back to the family Bible to recall a favourite engraving:

> Why couldn't we have seen
> this old Nativity while we were at it?
> – the dark ajar, the rocks breaking with light,
> an undisturbed, unbreathing flame,
> colorless, sparkless, freely fed on straw,
> and, lulled within, a family with pets,
> – and looked and looked our infant sight away.

A first impression is that the lines release something like a cry: why is it we can we no longer believe in this familiar Nativity scene, Mary, Joseph, the baby in the manger, the adoring animals? A second reading, and the phrase 'a family with pets' calls to mind the child Elizabeth who, in former days, would have pored over this illustration, filled with desire, particularly for the pets. A third reading suggests that Bishop has resolved her existential dilemma by escaping into art. If the engraving of the Nativity cannot be true, it can still be beautiful, and in memory its beauty is preserved. But finally we are drawn to the mystery of the last line: 'and look and look our infant sight away.' One can see, in a Wordsworthian sense, why Bishop might have wanted to look and look until she confirmed the strength of her 'infant sight'. But why would this poet – who preserved perfectly the all-observant eye of childhood – ever want to look it away? Did she mean that until we rid ourselves of false childish beliefs we will never grow up? Or did she mean that since 'infant sight' will disappear anyway, it is better to 'look' it away than to expel it logically? Elizabeth Bishop must have realized that her art and her pristine 'infant sight' were mutually dependent, and that her talent made it desirable for her, in certain respects, not to grow up. But suppose it were possible to retain a vision of something like 'truth' even though one had lost 'infant sight'? Suppose she were to look and look, harder and harder, at 'God's spreading fingerprint' in the book of life? Suppose she let her eye drop 'weighted' through those 'ripples above sand' and through the storms of her own dreamy imagination until it freed her into an intimation of knowledge? She might then be able to rise and walk calmly from the waiting room instead of falling out of it into 'cold blue-black space'.

Bishop herself probably could not have explained what she meant by 'look and look our infant sight away' any more than she would have wanted to analyse the *finale* of another magnificent poem, 'At the Fishhouses' – the last lines of which she said came to her in a dream. Nevertheless, the two poems end with revelations that move, first with a step and then with a giant stride, away from the fixed impressions of childhood. The Bulmer Bible's 'old Nativity' opens to 'the dark *ajar*'. The rocks are 'breaking with light' though their flame, undisturbed and unbreathing, consumes nothing, and the vision, though beautiful, is static. The final lines of 'At the Fishhouses' on the other hand, recreate the icy sea as a 'transmutation of fire', one that 'feeds on stones and burns with a dark grey flame.' In the last six lines, the poet in effect *does* look her infant sight away. Instead of longing for the stasis of a lasting myth, she perceives that knowledge is never permanent, that the ever-moving flames of the sea are

> dark, salt, clear, moving, utterly free,
> drawn from the cold hard mouth
> of the world, derived from the rocky breasts
> forever, flowing and drawn, and since
> our knowledge is historical, flowing, and flown.

This is an adult view of knowledge, informed by experience and recognized as 'free' precisely because no prettiness deflects it. The 'cold hard mouth of the world' suckles from no mythic Virgin, only from the 'rocky breasts' of eternally flowing time. With time flows, too, that precious childhood that the startling word 'flown' tells us has disappeared. Bishop's triumph in 'At the Fishhouses' was to achieve the hardness of scientific truth without having sacrificed anything of the poem's spirituality. Rarely, in any of her mature work, did Bishop came so close again to 'philosophising'. At Vassar she was less inhibited, and young Elizabeth Bishop's thoughts on time are therefore the subject of our next chapter.

CHAPTER TWO

Time's Andromeda

Time's in her pocket, ticking loud
on one stalled second . . .

'The Colder the Air'

I

Elizabeth Bishop's academic critics have for the most part con-
nected her work with her life, and it is true that in many respects
she was a writer 'whose life experiences shaped and mediated the
expression of her art.'[1] Yet the contents of her first collections,
North & South (1946) and *A Cold Spring* (1955), suggest that she
began as a poet of ideas. This is not to say that poems like 'The
Map', 'The Imaginary Iceberg', 'The Man-Moth', and 'The Gentle-
man of Shalott' are ideological; rather that they were influenced by
surrealism in a cultural climate that favoured aesthetic experimen-
tation. They come across, even today, as many-faceted dream-like
constructions that lend themselves to a variety of interpretations,
and this indeterminacy, if I can put it that way, is one source of
their charm. At the same time, their language, however unexpect-
edly imaginative, still pointedly relates to familiar 'things': maps
buildings, ships, mirrors, tears, bread, coffee.

'The Map' – with which the poet chose to open both *North &
South* and her 1955 volume – shows us the poet looking at a map
and transforming it into poetry. In short, 'The Map' represents a

three-fold process of imagination. First, in drawing his map, the map-maker had to revise the topography of the real world to produce an image of it. He created, in effect, a work of art. Next, the poet looking at this map, imaginatively interprets the map-maker's interpretation. In Elizabeth Bishop's eyes, the map becomes curiously alive. 'Or does the land lean down to lift the sea from under?/ Along the fine tan sandy shelf/ is the land tugging at the sea from under?' Finally, the reader of the poem, who knows nothing of this map except what the poet sees it as, responds to the poet's words, and to what these words reveal about her attitude to the map's projection.

The poet has something to say, evidently, about the nature of art and in 'The Map', particularly, about how looking at a picture of the world can humanise and domesticate it. 'We can stroke these lovely bays / under a glass as if they were expected to blossom.' And again, 'These peninsulas take the water between thumb and finger/ like women feeling for the smoothness of yard-goods.' When she concludes at the end that 'Mapped waters are more quiet than the [map's] land is', we see that the map-maker's art has reversed the natural state of these elements. 'Norway's hare runs south in agitation,/ profiles investigate the sea, where land is.' In the 1930s, Elizabeth Bishop was ostensibly writing poems about the act of seeing, imagining and creating works of art, though critics such as Victoria Harrison maintain that a good deal else, psychologically or subliminally, was going on in them.[2] I think it is fairer to take Elizabeth Bishop's word for it that 'The Map' was written about a real map she once owned in NewYork, letting subliminal interpretations alone until we have looked at what the poem literally says.

'The Imaginary Iceberg', which follows 'The Map' in all Bishop's selections, equally ponders the nature of imagination; but in this poem, Bishop's humanising hopes for art are questioned, even reversed. This iceberg, the coldest possible embodiment of the imagination, is preferred to the ship of comfortable, messy life even though, in its beauty, the iceberg perpetually threatens the ship with destruction. The two poems together set up an antithesis that Bishop may have preserved on purpose. In 'The Map' she implies that the map-maker's picture is kinder and more domestic than real land and water; the art of map-making renders nature acceptable. In 'The Imaginary Iceberg' her opening declaration that 'We'd rather have the iceberg than the ship' appears to mean that a 'real' untamed vision of nature will be the artist's choice at any price, 'although it meant the end of travel.' In 'The Map' the printer-artist lets the names of seashore towns run out to sea, experiencing 'the same excitement/ as when emotion too far exceeds its cause.' Real emotions in 'The Map' have been replaced by names (words) that can't hurt her. In 'The Imaginary Iceberg', the sailor-artists would give their eyes for their vision's capacity to destroy them. At the end of 'The Map', making geography is held to be superior to making history. At the end of 'The Imaginary Iceberg', a romantic vision of beauty, equated with something absolute and unhuman, has to be abandoned as 'the ship steers off/ where waves give in to one another's waves' and people resume their ordinary lives.

It seems, then, that these two poems never resolve a quarrel that is going on between four abstract contenders: call them nature, art, vision and necessity. 'The Map' shows us art (or craft) taming nature by falsifying it in such a way as to make it humanly comprehensible – and therefore delightful. 'The Imaginary Iceberg', on the other hand, says 'No, nature cannot ever be truly domesticated. Yet in the end, we can't live with the deadly truths that behoove our souls because human necessity (the social nature of the ship) always insists that we compromise.'

Something like this quarrel over the meaning of art, is, I believe, the underlying subject of a good many poems in *North & South*. If, in the 'The Imaginary Iceberg', the artist chooses the iceberg – a creation both of nature and imagination – over the ship, then the short lyric, 'Casabianca', burns up the ship. The boy standing on the burning deck is on fire with love. He tries to escape into poetry by reciting the childish lines of Mrs Hemans's 'The Boy Stood on the Burning Deck', but the love that has torched the ship is too much for him. He and the 'swimming sailors' would, of course, like to save themselves through elocution, but either the poem isn't good enough or the art of poetry itself, caught in the conflagration of love, never has a chance.

*   *   *

By the time Elizabeth Bishop was writing highly-wrought metaphorical fables like 'Casabianca' and its companion-piece, 'The Colder the Air', she had already served an apprenticeship under the seventeenth-century poets, George Herbert and Richard Crashaw, and chosen for a modern master the nineteenth-century Jesuit priest, Gerard Manley Hopkins. Although as an adult Elizabeth Bishop specifically rejected Christianity, her devout, unquestioning faith in certain works of art was in its nature spiritual. More than this, she deliberately chose for models poets who were dedicated to the forms and rituals of their beliefs. The handful of 'Poems Written in Youth' represented in the *Complete Poems* makes it evident that even before she went to Vassar, Elizabeth Bishop was seriously experimenting with words, rhythms and unexpectedly inventive ideas. The lyrics she completed while at college reveal a self-conscious young poet struggling to establish her own modernist style while relying heavily on Hopkins and the seventeenth century Metaphysicals. It seems that she was not much attracted by the Romantics, though at fifteen she had 'loved Shelly and Whitman'.[3] She certainly mocked, while at Vassar, any Edna St Vincent Millay-ish bent towards self-exploration. This anti-romantic streak gives Bishop's youthful productions an oddly unnatural tone, as if poetry challenged her as a method of verbal construction while offering her a sophisticated (and therefore justifiable) escape route out of herself.

Certainly no one who met Elizabeth Bishop in the early 1930s would have anticipated the homely, autobiographical turn her writing would take in the '50s and '60s. At Vassar, Elizabeth and four or five of her friends were unabashedly élitist. Excited by the idea of Modern Art and priding themselves on their advanced tastes, they chose to be seen as painters, musicians and writers of a superior caste whose imaginative gifts entitled them to look down on less aesthetically enlightened contemporaries. Names like Gertrude Stein, James Joyce, Schoenberg, Vuillard and Picasso tripped familiarly off their tongues. They even rather despised their politically left-wing classmates, adopting the attitude that art – because of its eternal nature – was essentially of more value than history. (Again, note the argument in 'The Map'.)

We get a sharpish picture of the nineteen-year-old poet from the report of a young teacher at Vassar in 1930 who, in accordance with the college's practice, wrote up one of the more interesting Freshmen. Replying to an enquiry from me in 1964, Barbara Swain remembered Elizabeth Bishop as 'an enormously cagey girl who looked at authorities with a suspicious eye and was quite capable of attending to her own education anyway.' Recalling her 'stooped walk, and her gimlet look from under her eyebrows,' Miss Swain admitted to liking this 'prickly' rebel who was 'evidently doomed to be a poet.'[4] Scholars have sometimes wondered why she put it just that way: *doomed*? But to Elizabeth Bishop 'doomed' might even then have seemed prescient. For by 1930, when Miss Swain was teaching Shakespeare to first-year English students, Elizabeth Bishop had already undergone and worked out techniques to contain that 'prize unhappy childhood' of which she almost never spoke, even to her closest associates.

Interviews with Frani Blough Muser and others among Elizabeth's friends at Walnut Hill School and Vassar tend to confirm Miss Swain's impression.[5] Out of their collective reminiscences, 'Bish' or 'Bysshe', as they called her, emerges as a girl with a powerful, though quiet, presence, set apart by her intelligence from most of the other girls, and determinedly superior. Proud, inventive, brilliant in English but full of bizarre whims, she was apt, when feeling uncomfortable, to take to the road like a tramp. Yet even as an adolescent, judging from these reports and from her letters of the period, young Miss Bishop appears to have been more amused than embittered by human folly. She comes across, on the whole, as a shy, often humorous tom-boy who affected a robust, even brash independence. School friends such as Barbara Chesney perceived that she was often unhappy. When caught off her intellectual high ground, she could be pathetically dependent. School and college authorities, appraised of her family history, showed considerable understanding – more, anyway, than the young Elizabeth Bishop would have credited them with. While she was at Walnut Hill, for instance, she was sent to a psychotherapist in Boston who hoped to clear away any repressions or fears regarding her mother that might be troubling her. Typically, Elizabeth 'refused to talk openly, and the meetings were soon discontinued.'[6]

At Vassar, as at Walnut Hill, Elizabeth seemed at first abnormally shy, shunning all public appearances and instantly renouncing her music studies when she found herself too nervous to perform on the piano. Yet by her third year she had established herself as a prime mover in an artists' coterie, one of five founders of a rebel literary magazine she, Mary McCarthy, Margaret Miller and two sisters, Eunice and Eleanor Clarke, started in defiance of the more conventional *Vassar Review*. The magazine, *Con Spirito* (so named not only because its writing was spirited but because its founders, enjoying themselves as conspiritors, met off campus in a speak-easy), published its third and last issue under Elizabeth in the fall term of her senior year. Mary McCarthy, Eunice Clarke and Elizabeth's closest friend Frani Blough had left Vassar in June of 1933 (this was the class on which Mary McCarthy later based her novel *The Group*). *Con Spirito*, for want of funds and new talent, soon merged with the *Vassar Review*,[7] but while it lasted, its modernist slant stirred up a good deal of debate. Authorship was anonymous, and though the faculty never approved, T. S. Eliot spoke well of it when Bishop interviewed him in May of 1933 for the student newspaper.

The poems Elizabeth Bishop chose to publish in *Con Spirito*'s first issue afterwards struck a student reviewer at Princeton as having some merit, though the young Arthur Mizener (as he turned out to be) thought they were imitative of Hopkins without showing understanding of Hopkins's metrics. Bishop, whose thorough analysis of Hopkins's meters would appear in the (renovated) *Vassar Review* in February 1934, instead of rebuffing her critic, complimented him. She herself may have realised that her 'Sonnets for the Eyes' were archaic and affected. Still, if they were bad, they were bad in an interesting way. The octet from Sonnet III, for instance, is typical. It appears to be playing Elizabethan-cum-Hopkins-like variations on the theme of the five senses, though like Bishop's later (lesbian) love poems, it hides its import behind an almost impenetrable thicket of images. (Some of this imagery crops up again in *North & South*.)

> Thy senses are too different to please me -
> Touch I might touch; whole the split difference
> On twenty fingers' tips. But hearing's thence
> Long leagues of thee, where wildernesses increase . . . See
> Flesh-forests, nerve-vined, pain-star-blossom full,
> Trackless to where trembles th' ears' eremite.
> And where from there a stranger turns to sight?
> Thine eyes nest, say, soft shining birds in the skull?

During her Junior year at Vassar, when the *Con Spirito* fever was at its height, Bishop submitted a baroque pastiche, 'Hymn to the Virgin' (a Virgin moth-eaten and fly-spotted after hundreds of 'storage years' in heaven's 'great attic'), to a contest sponsored by an avant-garde literary journal, *Hound & Horn*. Bishop's 'Virgin' and a story called 'Then Came the Poor' rated only an honourable mention in the competition, but the following summer the editor asked her for more work, which receiving, he passed on to the magazine's regional director, Yvor Winters. In October, Winters wrote to Bishop, offering her criticism and mentioning the name of a graduate student at Harvard with whom she might find it rewarding to correspond. Donald Stanford, at Harvard, had also heard from Winters, and he soon initiated the correspondence. Bishop's letters to Stanford show her thinking with a precosity and toughness that, in later years, she sometimes tried to play down.[8]

Like Arthur Mizener at Princeton, Stanford found 'Three Sonnets for the Eyes' and 'Hymn to the Virgin' obscure and too Hopkinsesque. Bishop's rhythms, compared to his own smooth iambics, seemed to him crude. This time Bishop wrote back defending her irregularities. She liked to distinguish between two different kinds of poetry, she said. One, like Stanford's, lay 'at rest' on the page; the other – the kind she was attempting – strove instead for 'action' within the poem. Quoting from an article, 'The Baroque Style in Prose' by M.W. Croll, she emphasised a discovery to which she had given a good deal of thought. This was that no idea can ever be set down in poetry once it has ceased to be experienced. The purpose of baroque writing, as she understood it, 'was to portray, not a thought, but a mind thinking.' The process of conceiving an idea had to be part of its meaning. Whatever the faults of her own verse, it did literally enact her thoughts.[9]

Stanford, doubtless, was impressed by all this without agreeing with her, and perhaps at first he sounded patronising. Towards the end of one letter (20 November 1933), Bishop scornfully lashed out at her correspondent's suggestion that her perceptions were 'almost impossible for a woman's.' 'Now what the hell,' she fumed, 'you know that's meaningless.'[10] It was a feminist stand she defended vigorously for the rest of her life. At the same time, she must sometimes have harboured reservations about the generality of women writers. When she sent Stanford two copies of Con Spirito, for example, she felt unsure enough of its merits to remark that for 'women's college writing' it was pretty good. 'Also,' she added, 'we decided to get rid of another curse of women's colleges – the awful emphasis on personality – and have it anonymous.'[11]

This combination of bold aggression and apologetic self-doubt – or at least, *apparent* self-doubt – was characteristic of Bishop when she was writing to someone she was not quite sure would understand her. All the same, the letters to Stanford were written by a young woman who never doubted that she had a right to hold literary opinions. The arguments she advanced complement an ingenious idea she had put forward the year before in two papers written for a Contemporary Fiction course. 'Time's Andromedas' and 'Dimensions for a Novel' set out to explore the nature of fictional time. From what she says in 'Dimensions for a Novel' about mistrusting 'bright ideas' about *how* to do things before doing the things themselves, it seems certain that Bishop expected to test her theory of what she called 'experience time' in writings of her own.[12]

*   *   *

'Time's Andromedas' (1933) sets out to be a study of the time dimension in the experimental novels of Dorothy Richardson and Gertrude Stein, though it opens with a descriptive passage no one could have written but Elizabeth Bishop. One day 'last fall', she begins, she was studying so hard that she had dug herself into a sort of thought-cave. Her own ideas, conflicting with those of the book she was reading, were 'making such a wordy racket' that she forgot where she was until she realised she was sitting with her back to a window, listening to sounds high in the air that she had been aware of, unconsciously, all day. A sunset was dyeing the pages of her book pink; the sounds were of birds crying as they migrated south. As she looked up, it flashed upon her that these birds (they were too high to identify) were utterly ignoring the fields, roads, houses and steeples over which they flew. Migrating according to instinctive, mathematical rules of their own, the birds' world was not her world, and their time was not her time.

Watching them carefully, she noticed that though their wings appeared to be beating in unison, some birds flew a little more swiftly, some more slowly than others. Yet they were moving as one, with the spaces between each bird making one pattern with the sky, the spaces between groups of birds, another. It came to her the next day (the migration was still in progress) that the flying birds, moving in their own time, were setting up different time patterns, 'all closely related, all minutely varied', yet all of them together forming something she would think of later as a static idea: the idea of the *migration*.

'What,' Bishop then asks, 'went to make up this peculiar passing of *another* time?' While she was watching the birds, her sense of time was theirs. And still, when she looked away, she was conscious for just a moment of their time, 'pulsing against and contradicting' her own. Then the migration lost its reality and became 'a fixed feeling, a little section of the past which had changed and become timeless.' Realising that the migrating birds were finally, for her, not a 'unit of motion, but rather a static point' as if frozen into the word 'migration', she wonders if traditional novels don't create their own time-systems, very much as migrating birds do. In a novel by Dickens or Hardy, the reader slips out of his or her own time and accepts the 'suppositious' time of the plot. Once the book has been read, though, its time-pattern becomes merely 'a condition', a fixed idea that is brought to mind when the book is remembered. Only with effort can we imagine its events and characters 'spread out in our own time-scheme.'

Contrasting her idea of time in traditional novels with that in experimental fictions by Marcel Proust, Virginia Woolf, James Joyce, Dorothy Richardson and Gertrude Stein, Bishop suggests that these modernists have either tried to construct a time-feeling *like* the reader's, but on a smaller scale; or else they have attempted to make their books' time appear continuous in real time. As an example of the first instance, Bishop looks at the opening to volume one of Dorothy Richardson's novel-sequence, *Pilgrimage*. Right away, she says, the heroine's stream-of-consciousness time is introduced into the reader's time without jarring it. Miriam has a past – the school days she is leaving behind her – and a future into which she will carry a trunk of memories when she sets out for a new life the next day. If the weight of pages in the reader's right hand represents that future, then Miriam's past life, too, will be revealed in it. Time throughout *Pilgrimage*, therefore, with its long 'loops' of digression out of the narrative into the protagonist's memory, *feels* like human time, though it is, of course, shorter.

Gertrude Stein, differing from Richardson, understood time only as a continuum of the present. In nearly a thousand pages of *The Making of Americans*, Bishop writes (a little tartly), Miss Stein gropes for a way of representing a 'continuous present' by employing 'curious tricks' – such as endlessly recapitulating passages and turning all her verbs into present participles. By manipulating syntax and grammar to produce the illusion of a time frozen in the present, Stein gives her reader no impression at all of her characters' 'presence'. Nobody she creates has a past – as actual people do have, and do remember.

Bishop (who admired Dorothy Richardson and was suspicious of Stein) nevertheless criticises both novelists for, as she puts it, looking too often at the hourglass. Quoting Wyndham Lewis, she accuses them of being 'timebound', adding that in giving the title 'Time's Andromedas' to her essay, she intended to point out the 'difficulties' inherent in such fiction. It is at this point, after having restated her thesis (Richardson and Stein as representing 'two distinct ideas of time in writing') that Bishop comes up with a stunning idea of her own. Is it possible, she speculates, that a sort of *experience-time* could be represented in fiction? Could characters be made to respond to time as people actually do? Events, she argues, don't really strike us as they arrive in a procession of days and hours. Sometimes we anticipate them, sometimes we forget them, sometimes it takes us months or years to realize an important event has happened. Comparing actual time-experiences to dropped coins that sink to the bottom of a pond at different speeds, she suggests that writers should imitate boys diving for them. Why shouldn't a novelist catch some days while leaving others to fall unnoticed? Why always set Tuesday before Wednesday and Thursday before Friday when a protagonist might experience Friday as completing something that happened on Tuesday and forget about Wednesday and Thursday altogether?

The idea of experience-time must have struck Elizabeth Bishop just as she was finishing 'Time's Andromedas', for soon afterwards she produced a second essay, 'Dimensions for a Novel', in which she explored it more fully. For an epigraph, she borrowed a line from Wallace Stevens: 'The lines are straight and swift between the stars', implying that in imagination, time has almost no duration. The mind leaps over time's spaces just as one's eyes, gazing at the night sky, travel millions of light years in an instant between one star and another. Invoking T. S. Eliot's idea of an order of 'literary monuments' in historical time, she claims that in ordinary life, too, every important new event changes the weight and perspective of all the other events in one's past.

For a girl in her early twenties, this was an astounding insight, though if she tried to put it to the test in that early aborted novel, it seems she failed to meet the demands of her own modernist standards. Maybe she found that, in practice, experience-time bound her into a time-theory just as inhibiting as Dorothy Richardson's or Gertrude Stein's. More likely, her imagination encountered an impenetrable block when it attempted to dart back to periods in her past. How was she to bring to mind those awful images of her mother's madness? Or all those miserable months of lying in bed with asthma? And how on earth, in a story, was she to scrutinise the truth of her homosexual longings?

So far as I know Elizabeth Bishop rarely, if ever, referred to experience-time after she left Vassar, yet twenty years later she succeeded wonderfully – and to her great surprise – in recreating a timeless present in 'Gwendolyn' and 'In The Village'. In the 1930s she felt safer turning abstract ideas into fables in the manner of Poe and Hawthorne. Two brilliant, cryptic little tales – 'The Sea & Its

Shore' (1937) and 'In Prison' (1938) – shimmer with that very quality of ideas-being-enacted that Bishop said she valued in baroque poetry. The drunken Edwin Boomer (a common spelling of Bulmer in Nova Scotia), picking up 'literature' on the beach to read and burn in his shack by the ocean, may have been suggested by her Uncle Arthur, but he is more idea than man. So is the reclusive narrator of 'In Prison', meditating on the difference between Choice and Necessity as he plans the perfect escape from life's disorders and his own undesired, mostly unpleasant emotions. It is possible to see these parables as satirical *jeux d'esprit*, written to entertain Bishop's sophisticated friends. More profoundly, they reflect their author's strong suspicion and dislike of her own feelings. Why in her youth did she choose to write so much about socially isolated madmen? And why are they always men, not women? As fictional figures, are they really as pleased with themselves as they sound, or are they bravely making the best of intolerable conditions? Isn't the human condition itself unbearable? In which case, aren't these outsiders something like characters in plays by Samuel Beckett: bound into time but free in their knowledge of necessity and in many ways better off than their fellow humans who know nothing of their ineluctable entrapment?

When 'In Prison' appeared in *The Partisan Review* in March 1938, one of its severest critics was Marianne Moore, whom Elizabeth had met shortly before she graduated from Vassar. Miss Moore's famous 'taking up' of Miss Bishop in 1934, just two months before Gertrude Bulmer Bishop died in a state sanatorium in Nova Scotia, probably affected Bishop's decision to settle in New York rather than Boston, where it seems she thought for a while of studying medicine.[13] Family factors, too, may have prejudiced her against Massachusetts. News of her mother's death, coming just as she was preparing to graduate from Vassar, must have upset her, though at the time she kept her mother's history a secret. As Bishop had anticipated in her theory of experience-time, she began to realise what her mother had meant to her only when she found herself writing about her Nova Scotia childhood in Brazil; that was in 1952.

David Kalstone, among other critics, has speculated that because Marianne Moore lived permanently with *her* mother, the motherless Elizabeth Bishop would have found in their delightful, eccentric apartment at 260 Cumberland Street in Brooklyn two mothers to make up for the one she had lost. And of course, the Moores did frequently offer her affectionate, if firmly intellectual, hospitality. They also undertook to scrutinise and correct the poems and stories Elizabeth (often self-deprecatingly) submitted to them – though it seems that, despite the diplomacy of her letters, Bishop usually went her own way and wrote as she pleased. In suggesting that Marianne Moore became, for a time, Miss Bishop's literary mother, Kalstone also pointed out that Elizabeth, for that very reason, would, in some part of her, have wanted to defy her.[14]

After Marianne Moore died in February 1972, Elizabeth Bishop drafted a memoir, 'Efforts of Affection', published in *Vanity Fair* in June 1983, and later reprinted in the *Collected Prose*. Explaining her choice of title, Bishop informs her readers that Moore's *Collected Poems* of 1951 included a poem called 'Efforts and Affection'. This title Marianne Moore herself had altered to 'Efforts *of* Affection' in the copy she gave to her friend. 'I liked this change very much,' Bishop continues, 'and so I am giving the title 'Efforts of Affection' to the whole piece.' What is not explained is why both these gifted women regarded affection as a feeling unnatural enough to require 'effort'. A certain wariness on the part of the older poet may have been engendered by a little condescension on the part of the younger. That Marianne Moore 'knew best' was tacitly agreed between them; yet Miss Bishop belonged to a fresh, assertive generation of women graduates with less sense of duty than Miss Moore's, and she very likely had no more idea of slavishly following Marianne Moore's lead in poetry than she had of incarcerating herself in a city apartment for the rest of her life.

Marianne Moore had a great deal to teach her, certainly, but she was not capable of understanding all the ways in which Elizabeth Bishop proposed to develop her talent.

II

The New York City into which Elizabeth Bishop and many of her Vassar classmates debouched in the Depression year of 1934–35 was a hotbed of radical politics fuelled by enthusiasm – at least on the part of the college-educated young – for social revolution, European travel, modern art and experimental theatre. Mary McCarthy's novel, *The Group* (1954), catches the spirit of the era very well, but Elizabeth Bishop, too, touches on its mood in city poems like 'From the Country to the City' and 'Letter to N.Y.' and in that amused miniature, 'The USA School of Writing', based on her first badly paid, pseudonymous job with a decidedly shadey correspondence school.

As this New York memoir suggests, the social attitudes she and her coevals adopted were fairly inconsistent: the girls were 'pink' yet privileged, sophisticated yet amateur, ambitious yet naïve. As Vassar intellectuals, Frani Blough, Mary McCarthy, Margaret Miller and Bishop herself set forth boldly to conquer New York and make names for themselves in the arts, settling in bohemian quarters in down-town Greenwich Village and attending lectures at New York University and Columbia between trips to chamber concerts, the theatre, the Metropolitan Museum and the Museum of Modern Art. Mary McCarthy Johnsrud gave literary parties, courting the editors of *The Nation* and *The Partisan Review*. In the autumn of 1935, when Elizabeth was exploring Paris and Frani Blough, having already sampled Europe, was studying music at the New School in New York, the two planned to collaborate in the writing of a masque in the style of Ben Jonson; or perhaps it would be a chamber opera that began with 'a few select people sitting around after dinner improvising an entertainment.'[15] It was important, they told each other, that their collaboration should be free of Wagnerian seriousness; they would produce 'something. . . funny and amusing, not heavy.' Meanwhile, Margaret Miller, studying Fine Art in New York, was considering writing a thesis on Inigo Jones and the Italian baroque in England. They were all of them intelligent and gifted young women, more innocent than they thought they were, full of plans for a cultured, revolutionary future in which they should and would be recognised (hadn't they been educated at Vassar?) as the equals of men.

At the same time, it has to be said that these brightest and best of Vassar graduates were, of necessity, cut off from the mainstream of American life by the exclusive, single-sex nature of their education and by their high social expectations. Vassar, in the first third of the century, was a more self-enclosed upper-class college than it is today, and its graduates were, many of them, extremely wealthy. Louise Crane, with whom Elizabeth toured Europe in 1935 and again in 1937, was the daughter of a paper-millionaire-cum-US Senator whose widow – ruling from a vast apartment on 5th Avenue – was a noted patroness and trustee of the Museum of Modern Art. Though Louise was no intellectual – she never did get her degree from Vassar – she was an excellent judge of modern painting, and, further to Elizabeth's taste, a girl of apparently unlimited self-confidence and energy. She lived to enjoy herself, to sail, fish, drink, attend jazz concerts and, like her mother, patronise artists. Elizabeth, always attracted by humour and high spirits, found in Louise an amusing friend and, in due course, a lover.

For, after leaving Vassar, the young poet had found herself more alone than ever. Despising the tastes of her Bishop relatives (her uncle Jack, in any case, died in 1935, bequeathing her enough money to buy a clavichord) and with no idea of returning to rural Nova Scotia, she settled into a tiny apartment that Mary McCarthy and her playwright husband found for her near Greenwich Village. The city as a whole was sick with the miseries of the Great

Depression; unemployment and trades union agitation were rife.
Yet it was Bishop's own depressions – those moments of black
dread she recorded in bewilderment in her notebooks – that,
together with recurring asthma attacks, made her more than
ordinarily dependent on her Vassar connections. Marianne
Moore's stalwart advocacy proved invaluable, but it was not
enough. Although in 1935 Marianne Moore chose three of her
poems (including 'The Map') for an introductory anthology called
Trial Balances and recommended her protegée to Horace Gregory,
editor of Life and Letters Today, Bishop remained shy and self-
critical – dissatisfied, chiefly, with her slow pace of production.
With introductions to influential editors flowing in, too, from
Mary McCarthy and Louise Crane, Elizabeth Bishop should have
felt encouraged by her New York literary debut. Instead, she often
felt inferior or mentally paralysed.

Very likely behind her psychological troubles lay the uncomfort-
able fact of her sexual orientation. Teenage girls often go through
a stage of falling in love with their women teachers or with older
girls they admire, but in Bishop's case such 'crushes' obviously
went deeper. And while most of her school and college friends were
probably, like Frani Blough, bright girls who simply shared her gifts
and interests, it seems that at Vassar, Elizabeth did fall in love with
her roommate, Margaret Miller.[16]

Perhaps her struggle to control her homosexual yearnings led
her, during her Vassar years, to encourage the advances of a
sensitive young man named Robert Seaver. Seaver was a graduate
of Hamilton College and Harvard Business School who, crippled
by polio, had found work in a bank in Pittsfield, Massachusetts. He
seems to have fallen in love with Elizabeth, hoping that her hunger
for affection would persuade her to marry him. Evidently she liked
him and shared his tastes. They may even have come to some
understanding in 1933 or 1934. But in the summer of 1935,
Elizabeth sailed to France with a younger Vassar graduate, Harriet
Tompkins, after having turned Seaver down. In November of 1936,

when Bishop was back in New York and her relationship with Louise Crane was well-established, Seaver (it is assumed) committed suicide. Before he shot himself he sent Elizabeth Bishop a postcard on which he had written 'Elizabeth, Go to Hell!'. The effect on Elizabeth Bishop of such an accusation at such a time can be imagined. Had she ever allowed Seaver to hope that some day he might succeed with her? Seaver's sister thought not. Bishop had been fond of her brother, but she had told him before she left for France that she was never going to marry.[17]

Whatever the reasons for Seaver's suicide – there could well have been many – Elizabeth Bishop evidently felt partly responsible. Her feelings of guilt were not assuaged, either, by a further tragedy that occurred the following summer, this time involving Margaret Miller. In June of 1937, Elizabeth and Louise Crane set off on a second European tour, starting in Ireland and meeting up with Margaret Miller in London. By July all three were in France, touring the baroque churches of Burgundy in a car hired by Louise Crane. As they were driving back to Paris, a large car overtook them, forcing the girls off the road. Their car overturned, throwing them all out. Elizabeth and Louise got up shaken but unhurt; Margaret's right arm had been severed below the elbow. Her bleeding was stopped by a tourniquet tied by a local workman, and luckily the driver who had forced them off the road returned to drive Margaret to the nearest town. After four nightmare days of archaic medical treatment and interviews with the French police, Margaret was transferred to the American Hospital in Paris. From a hotel near the hospital, Elizabeth telephoned Margaret's mother in New York, but not wanting to alarm her, told her only half the truth. Mrs Miller, supposing that her daughter had only broken her arm, arrived on the scene early in August. Seeing what had really happened, she fainted, and then was furious with Elizabeth for not informing her immediately that Margaret had lost half her right arm.[18]

At first, Margaret made the best of the situation, but when complications set in after a skin-graft, she lost her will to recover and go on travelling. Elizabeth, who blamed Margaret's withdrawal on Mrs Miller's over-anxious attentions, was all this time suffering from severe asthma – no doubt the consequence of a complex of guilty self-accusations. By mid-September the crisis looked to be over. Margaret Miller remained depressed but she was out of hospital, and while they were waiting for a French trial, all four women rented an apartment on the Ile de Saint Louis. Elizabeth, with cheerful *sang-froid*, reported these events to Marianne Moore. To Frani Blough she wrote frankly of her growing impatience with Mrs Miller. By the end of November, with the trial successfully behind them, Elizabeth Bishop and Louise Crane fled to Rome. In December, having heard nothing from the Millers in Paris, they embarked for Boston and New York.

* * *

Elizabeth Bishop's letters of this period (1934–8), energetically written from addresses in New York, Paris, Brittany, Morocco, Spain, Florida, Paris again and Italy, pretty well cover the period of her first flowering as a poet and story-writer. By the autumn of 1937, she had published, with Marianne Moore's encouragement, at least thirteen poems in magazines (*Poetry, The Nation, Partisan Review*) and two stories – one of which, 'The Baptism', would be chosen for *Best Stories of 1937*. Since Bishop's self-censoring aesthetic conscience would have cut short, at this time, any attempt to write poetry that confessed to personal anguish, poems like 'Love Lies Sleeping' and 'Sleeping Standing Up' can be understood, at least in part, as coded messages imparted to her consciousness through her dreams.

At the same time, some of Bishop's early, quasi-surrealist poems reveal a mind so preoccupied with the act of thinking that they virtually leave no room for displays of feeling. 'Paris, 7 A.M.' and 'Quai d'Orleans', placed side by side in her first collection, date from those two very different trips to France, and they show her writing from opposed sides of herself. In 'Paris, 7 A.M.', the poet follows every turn of her mind as it experiments with what looks like experience-time. The poem is set in a clock-crammed apartment near the Luxembourg Gardens that Louise Crane was renting, through her mother, from a Comtesse de Chambrun in the autumn and winter of 1935–6. The sadder, more personal 'Quai d'Orleans' – dedicated to Margaret Miller – is a lament, almost an elegy, composed after their car accident during the autumn of 1937. A reader has to realise how much, in the later poem, the speaker envies the *insensibility* of the Seine barges, trailing dead, insensible 'real leaves' in their leaf-shaped wakes. In a letter to Frani Blough (9 August 1937) Bishop burst out, 'I long for an Arctic climate where no emotions of any sort can possibly grow.' It was while she was struggling to nullify her strong feelings at this time that she accepted defeat in the poem's last despairing lines: 'If what we see could forget us half as easily,/ I want to tell you,/ as it does itself – but for life we'll not be rid / of the leaves' fossils.' By emphasising the unbridgeable distance between lifeless objects or 'things' and the sufferings of human beings, 'Quai d'Orleans' prefigures the softening and humanizing sympathy that warms so much of Bishop's later work. In the 1930s, 'Quai d'Orleans' is remarkable for being one of a very few poems that, however obliquely, expresses personal grief.

In contrast, 'Paris, 7 A.M.' – written two years earlier– scarcely lets an emotion squeeze through the fancy-work of its facade. Characteristically, Bishop plunges into her poem in the present tense, putting into practice her theories both of experience-time and of a mind acting out ideas as they occur. The speaker has just woken up, and we catch her making 'a trip' to each of many clocks in the apartment, all of which tell a different time. 'Time is an Étoile', she says, a star made of clock hands all pointing in different directions, like the Étoile of streets in the centre of Paris within its circles of suburbs. The focus then switches to a view of the pale Paris sky which resembles, she thinks, a pigeon's wing. The image is immediately revised to 'a dead wing with damp feathers' as the poet first looks out the window into the courtyard below, and then at the mansard roofs with their ornamental urns and live pigeons. Her view of Paris, together with her clock-given idea of star-shapes within circles, remind her of snowy New England or Nova Scotian winters, of snow-forts she helped build as a child and of piled up snowballs with their 'star-splintered hearts of ice'. 'Hearts of ice' could give rise to worrying resonances, but her mind won't stop to consider them; it has instead flashed back to the 'dead pigeon' which is also 'the sky from which a dead one fell.' And so the poem pulls to an end as the visionary moment of waking disintegrates into a series of useless questions. Have the urns caught the pigeon's ashes or his feathers? Did the star dissolve, or was it captured by the geometry of the city's squares and circles? 'Can the clocks say; is it [the star] there below,/ about to tumble in snow?'

Clearly, 'Paris, 7 A.M.' is related to the baroque experiments – 'Three Sonnets for the Eyes', 'Hymn to the Virgin', 'Three Valentines' – of Bishop's Vassar years. It is easier to 'solve' than those cluttered attempts, less imitative and plainer as to meaning. Still, it seems to be more an exercise than a poem. Its subject is certainly not Paris, nor the oddities of the 'apartment' (a word Bishop justified to Marianne Moore as being importantly something 'in parts') but the nature of time and memory. Clocks that cannot agree on *the* time make a Stevens-like star-figure that might contain *all* time. It is this star, together with the figure of the fallen pigeon, that forms a visual nexus out of which is projected yet a further image, that of a shadowy, long ago snow-fort piled with snowballs. Somehow the cleverness of all this, like a three-part invention in music or a Magritte painting, is, too, the poem's subject.

More verbal play with sets of sense-impressions form the basis of two other 'conceited' lyrics in *North & South*: 'The Colder the Air' and 'Wading at Wellfleet' – the latter arising from girlhood memories of a summer sailing camp on Cape Cod. To compare a glittering sea to a chariot with bladed wheels or to write of icy weather as a huntress whose arrows never miss and then to pile up images so as to support the weight of these metaphors: these were stunts that Bishop at the time enjoyed performing and performed well. And yet, the brilliance of such 'curious tricks' might have caused Donald Stanford, had he seen them, consternation. When, if ever, would she condescend to be serious?

Well, Bishop might have replied, 'The Map' and 'The Imaginary Iceberg' are serious, and then after a few light, baroque interludes, I returned at least to a kind of seriousness in 'Chemin de Fer'. The question is, can you, Donald Stanford, understand 'Chemin de Fer'? Read it several times. Do its tropes begin to make sense?

A Harvard-trained reader like Stanford might have noticed, even as a young man, that the fable has been put into the past tense – unusual for a poet who liked to keep her experience-time rolling through the present. Why a distancing past tense in this case alone? And if it literally refers to a walk on a railroad, why the 'pounding heart'? He probably would not have speculated, though, that the mystery clears up if we read 'Chemin de Fer' as an allegory either of lesbian love-making or (as I suspect) of female masturbation. Look at it again. The track on which the speaker says she was walking 'alone' was badly constructed. Like her own attempts at loving others, 'The ties [note the *double entendre*; 'sleepers' are called 'ties' in America] were too close together / or maybe too far apart.' The second stanza describes, without any hint of pornography, the 'scenery' of a woman's genitals: foliage of scrub-pine and oak hide a 'little pond' where the 'dirty hermit' lives. The pond looks like a tear (a recurring image in Bishop) holding onto too-familiar 'injuries'. In such a context the hermit's shooting off his 'shot gun', the ripple over the pond and his screaming 'Love should be put into action' hardly need explaining. The pet(ted) hen cries 'chook-chook' as an echo tries to confirm that putting *this* sort of love into action is natural and justified. Altogether, with its piston-like rhythms, the poem gives an impression at once of triumph and guilt. Moreover, it is just the sort of clever, truly hermetic verse that Elizabeth Bishop would have enjoyed writing in the '30s and '40s. Its meaning would have been obvious to those few with whom she shared her secrets, while to others, including the ever-watchful Miss Moore, it would present only an enigmatic parable of indeterminate import. While 'Chemin de Fer' does lend itself to interpretations such as I have suggested, we needn't make too much of them. Unlike many less inhibited (less witty) women poets today, Bishop wanted her private life kept private. It is probably significant that the central figure or speaker in most of these fable-like poems is either male or unspecified as to sex. I suspect, though, that she deliberately avoided speaking as a woman, not so much because she felt sexually ambiguous as because she wished to express psychological ideas that might not have been taken seriously had she declared an interest in gender. Look, for example, at 'The *Gentleman* of Shalott'. Here again is a fable the tone of which is not serious, and yet second and third readings reveal unsuspected depths. A fantasy based on the physical phenomenon of bilateral symmetry is seen really to be addressing a psychological 'split'. Bishop's gentleman is not Tennyson's *Lady* of Shalott, doomed to a double life, one outside and the other inside the looking-glass, but a divided or half *man* whose other half is pure mirror, i.e. pure speculation. The mirror either stands for this gentleman's idea-making faculties or (more likely) it represents his unconscious mind, the source of his dreams. To be whole, our gentleman has to live on both sides of his looking-glass, and of course the danger of the glass's slipping is an occupational hazard. One sees that the gentleman's predicament is again that of the artist forever making adjustments between two mental states; not only between the imaginary iceberg and the socially more comfortable ship, but between the conscious and unconscious components of a divided psyche. It is just this psychological 'sense of constant readjustment' that he finds 'exhilarating', though 'he wishes to be quoted as saying at present:/ "Half is enough" '. (Which half? one wonders at the end.)

Like 'The Imaginary Iceberg', then, 'The Gentleman of Shalott' can be read as a parable of the modern artist's precarious situation. Bishop set up alone in New York, remember, at a time when aspiring intellectuals were taking Freud very seriously and 'sicknesses of the soul' were being defined in the highly suggestive language of psychoanalysis. In those days, as often later, Elizabeth Bishop never ceased to live in the shadow of her mother's madness. From time to time Bishop did consult a Freudian therapist, and it appears she was sometimes helped. Yet it seems unlikely that the images of self-division that throng so many poems in North & South originated in this way. Reading carefully through *Poems: North & South – A Cold Spring*, we soon realise that while many poems directly or indirectly have to do with the nature of art and the divided creature who is the artist, these overlap with a more obscure series set in a twilight land between sleeping and waking – on the edge of the glass that divides dreams from conscious life.*

As we have seen, there were reasons why Elizabeth Bishop would have felt divided as a young woman. Though she never said so, behind all these early poems there lay a submerged, very painful struggle for 'readjustment' – or even sanity – that, like her own imaginary iceberg, occasionally took the form of a dazzling, all but irresistible invitation to self-destruction. Perhaps the closest she came to letting the glass slip and losing, as it were, half of herself found expression in the New York poem, 'Love Lies Sleeping'. Like 'Paris, 7 A.M.' it takes place as the speaker wakes

* See, for example, 'Love Lies Sleeping', 'The Weed', 'Paris, 7 A.M.', 'Sleeping on the Ceiling', 'Sleeping Standing Up', the third and fourth 'Songs for a Coloured Singer', 'Anaphora', 'Insomnia' and two out of four of the half-stiffled love poems towards the end of *A Cold Spring*. A prelude to all these can be found in the uncollected sonnet, 'Some Dreams They Forget' (1933). This suggests that dead birds falling and turning into tears were for a long time images in one of Bishop's recurring nightmares.

in the early morning and looks out the window at a city 'carefully' revealing itself. The imagery again turns on Bishop's habitual figures of stars and trains:

> Earliest morning switching all the tracks
> that cross the sky from cinder star to star,
> coupling the ends of streets
> to trains of light.

As daylight gradually banishes the 'hangover moons' of the night's neon signs, New York is new-born in the 'delicate over-workmanship' of its facades, so that the city, growing up into the watery summer sky resembles a chemical garden coloured 'pale blue, blue-green and brick.' Focussing on images, half dream-like, half-real, Bishop draws us into her poem with a recital of tiny events: sparrows begin 'their play'; something ominous in the distance goes 'Boom!' and leaves a cloud of smoke; a hand takes a shirt off a line; the water-wagon appears, its spray drying 'light-dry, dark-wet, the pattern / of the cool watermelon.' All this Bishopian bric-a-brac, though, creates no more than a setting for the unexpected crisis that takes place towards the end. Addressing the 'queer cupids of all persons getting up / whose evening meal they will prepare all day,' the speaker begs these love-spirits to be gentle with the hearts they feed on. 'Scourge them with roses only,' she pleads, 'be light as helium,'

> for always to one, or several, morning comes,
> whose head has fallen over the edge of his bed,
> whose face is turned
> so that the image of
>
> the city grows down into his open eyes
> inverted and distorted. No. I mean
> distorted and revealed,
> if he sees it at all.

In a letter of 8 January 1964, Bishop told me she thought this man in whose open eyes the city 'grows down' was dead. But who is he? Why should his 'cupid' have fed upon his heart to such excess? Did failed love drive him to suicide? Or is he a surrogate Elizabeth Bishop, drunk and divided from himself, a defeated Gentleman of Shalott whose glass has slipped and who has crossed the line between sleeping and waking, dreaming and consciousness, madness and sanity, once too often? Although the last lines of the poem are delivered with a sort of shrug, they are terribly disturbing. The idea that a city inverted and distorted is really *revealed* is a fearful indictment. Is the city revealed as corrupt and corrupting? Or does the word 'inverted' imply a sexual inversion? In the end, the reader feels that somebody or something has been found out, although it is impossible to say just who or what.

'Love Lies Sleeping' in many ways makes a pair with a lyric from *A Cold Spring* called 'Insomnia' in which 'inversion' is similarly important. To 'the moon in the bureau mirror' who 'looks out a million miles', everything real in the world is 'inverted'. Unquestionably a love poem, the lyric sounds like a folk-song; and like a folk-song in a minor key, its simplicity bespeaks unhappiness:

> So wrap up care in a cobweb
> and drop it down the well
>
> into that world inverted
> where left is always right,
> where the shadows are really the body,
> where we stay awake all night,
> where the heavens are shallow as the sea
> is now deep, and you love me.

Towards the end of a long letter dated 23 March 1964, Bishop mused, 'I sometimes wish I could recover the dreamy state of consciousness I lived in' (in the '30s and '40s), adding that, since coming to Brazil, she had learned 'a great deal more' about the world and its politics; yet she thought dreamy ignorance was better for her work. It is true that after 1952 the character of her poetry changed. Whatever horror lay hidden under the weird surfaces of her New York poems appears to have worked itself out and (almost) disappeared. The poetry she wrote in Key West, Florida (the 'south' of her title *North & South*) was likewise – as we shall see – of a different character. It hardly needs saying that places enormously affected her. As a place, New York was Bishop's 'city of dreadful night', yet she was for a long time dependent on it, nourished by its poisons as Baudelaire was nourished by the *demi monde* of Paris. Without knowing New York – without feeling it in her bones – Bishop could never have written 'The Man-Moth' or her stunningly clever sestina, 'A Miracle for Breakfast'.

'The Man-Moth' as Bishop often remarked, originated in a newspaper misprint for 'mammoth'. Though it may have taken the poet into unintended depths of herself, it is patently a poem about New York, or rather about how New York creates its own type of 'hopeful monster'. The poem begins with a sort of comic-book sketch of 'Man', a grown up, diminished, unobservant creature who lives 'above' ground in his city of 'battered moonlight' where his shadow 'lies at his feet like a circle for a doll to stand on.' Contrasted with this dull, upright, unseeing human doll, is his alter-ego, the Man-Moth, an alien, insect-like creature of whose existence Man is almost always unaware. The Man-Moth lives underground, only rarely paying visits to the surface, but when he does, he imagines the moon 'is a small hole at the top of the sky,/ proving the sky quite useless for protection.' As we follow this moth-child (another unbeliever) 'up the facades' of the skyscrapers, 'his shadow dragging like a photographer's cloth behind him,' we almost hope he will succeed in being forced through the moonhole 'in black scrolls on the night.' Frustrated in his pursuit of this ego-less heaven, the Man-Moth has to return 'to the pale subways of cement he calls his home.' There he seats himself in the train (Bishop's train, again) always 'facing the wrong way.' As the subway carries him backwards at a terrible speed though 'artificial tunnels', he dreams 'recurrent dreams', not daring to look out the window at the third rail, 'the unbroken draught of poison' which he regards 'as a disease [Sexuality? Suicide?] he has inherited the susceptibility to.'

Among the mysterious attributes of the Man-Moth is an eye in which trembles a single tear. The poem ends with a wonderful concatenation of images and sounds:

> Then from the lids
> one tear, his only possession, like the bee-sting, slips.
> Slyly he palms it, and if you're not paying attention
> he'll swallow it. However if you watch, he'll hand it over,
> cool as from underground springs and pure enough
>   to drink.

What are we to make of this dream-like allegory? A fable of the unconscious? A parable that shows the suppressed child in each of us receding through the 'artificial tunnels' of a misconceived past – a past we humans appear to control, but which in fact controls us? And then that 'one tear', the ManMoth's 'only possession'? Isn't this single drop of water the only element through which urban man and his Man-Moth double can – oh so rarely – communicate? Don't we all live in an adult present insecurely built over the tunnels of childhood? If this is so, then the Man-Moth's tear, cooled in underground springs of innocence and still, miraculously, 'pure enough to drink', represents the one hope that remains of escaping the living death of the city.

In preparing her first collection, Elizabeth Bishop carefully placed 'The Man-Moth' before the more difficult 'Love Lies Sleeping'; the sestina, 'A Miracle for Breakfast' came next. Marianne Moore had been critical of the 'Miracle' when she saw it in 1937, objecting to, among other things, the likeness in sound of the end-words 'sun' and 'crumb'. In her reply, Bishop apologised for the 'fault' but did nothing to correct it, pleading that the sestina was a 'stunt', and that in it she had tried to combine plain with unusual words in a new way.[19] She must have known that the sestina, experiment or not, was a tremendous achievement. Much later, in an interview with Ashley Brown published in 1966, Bishop was again dismissive of her 'Miracle': 'Oh, that's my depression poem,' she said. 'It was written shortly after the time of souplines and men selling apples, around 1936 or so.'[20] Indeed, the sestina seems to have originated in a dream-like event that might have happened in New York about that time. In a notebook she was keeping through the winter of 1934–5, Bishop recorded 'A Little Miracle'.

This morning I discovered I had forgotten to get any bread and I had only one dry crust for breakfast. I was resigning myself to orange juice and coffee . . . when the doorbell rang, I pushed the button, and up the stairs trailed a wary-looking woman, shouting ahead of herself: 'I don't want to *sell* you anything I want to give you something!' I welcomed her at that, and was presented with a small box containing three slices of 'Wonder Bread' all fresh, a rye, a white, and whole-wheat. Also a miniature loaf of bread besides – The only thing I disliked about the gift was that the woman opened the box, held it under my nose, and said 'Smell how sweet!' But I breakfasted on manna – . [21]

The words 'Wonder Bread' must have seeded themselves in Elizabeth's imagination to flower later into the Eucharistic drama that is almost impossible to miss in 'A Miracle for Breakfast', though Bishop herself denied that she consciously meant to refer to the Christian sacrament:

> At six o'clock we were waiting for coffee,
> waiting for coffee and the charitable crumb
> that was going to be served from a certain balcony,
> – like kings of old, or like a miracle.
> It was still dark. One foot of the sun
> steadied itself on a long ripple in the river.

Though yet another poem set at dawn, 'A Miracle for Breakfast' does without the usual Bishopian undercurrent of doubt or mistrust. The wisdom it dispenses is at first practical, advising the receivers of 'one lone cup of coffee' and 'one roll' to make the most of what they are given, to accept, as it were, the miracle of daily bread. The true miracle, however, is one that is enacted towards the end by the poet, and this, as she hastens to inform us, 'was not a miracle', not an act of charity nor an act of God, but an act of imagination performed 'with one eye close to the crumb':

> A beautiful villa stood in the sun
> and from its doors came the smell of hot coffee.
> In front, a baroque white plaster balcony
> added by birds, who nest along the river . . .
>
> and galleries and marble chambers. My crumb
> my mansion, made for me by a miracle,
> through ages, by insects, birds, and the river
> working the stone . . .

So the miracle Elizabeth Bishop had for breakfast was imaginary, an imaginary bread-crumb – not an iceberg – 'made through ages, by insects, birds, and the river/ working the stone.' And in this humbler form, the object imagined represents a means of identifying with life, or the makings and unmakings of life through the ages in nature's or geography's time. Although 'A Miracle for Breakfast' was an early, New York poem, it reconciled, however temporarily, the poet's impulse to sacrifice the world for art with her counter-impulse to see in the world the miracle that is always at hand, always available for inspection. All any of us need do is look.

CHAPTER THREE

Living with the Animals

I think I could turn and live with animals, they are
                so placid and self-contained,
I stand and look at them long and long.

They do not sweat and whine about their condition,
They do not lie awake in the dark and weep for their sins,
They do not make me sick discussing their duty to God,
Not one is dissatisfied, not one is demented with the
                mania of owning things,
Not one kneels to another, nor to his kind that lived
                thousands of years ago,
Not one is respectable or unhappy over the whole earth.

So they show their relations to me and I accept them,
They bring me tokens of myself, they evince them plainly
                in their possession.
                Walt Whitman, *Song of Myself*

Walt Whitman's long look at the animals was one of many ways in which his poetry challenged convention, for the most common use poetry has found for creatures throughout civilized history has not been naturalistic but allegorical or fabulistic. Ever since Aesop in the sixth century BC set a precedent of personifying animals and placing them in parodic human situations, the fable has stood its ground among literary genres. The homiletics of La Fontaine, for example, do not become very much more modern in Marianne Moore's (curiously awkward) translations. For as long as animal stories are read, Peter Rabbit, Br'er Fox and Mr Toad will continue to amuse the world's children. As for their elders, the aims of political satirists have been especially well served by animal allegory (viz. Orwell's Animal Farm), while specifically topical verse fables like *The Hind and the Panther* have long survived the circumstances they were designed to criticise. And just as Chaucer's *Nun's Priest's Tale* and *Parliament of Fowls* drew from a tradition of nature parables that extended far back into the Middle Ages, so equally do modern classics such as *The Wind in the Willows*, *Watership Down* and indeed Disney's *Micky Mouse* and *Tom and Jerry* cartoons owe their universal appeal to a convention so familiar that it is everywhere taken for granted.

Elizabeth Bishop, who loved animals and wrote charming letters describing her cats and her toucan, Uncle Sam, seems not to have been unhappy with the fabulistic tradition. She certainly approved of Beatrix Potter whose illustrated tales she often gave to children; she even experimented with creature-fables herself in short prose pieces. But she did, too, feel uneasy about exploiting a convention that took so little notice of the nature of animals themselves. 'The Fish', 'The Armadillo' and 'The Moose' remain fresh and endlessly rereadable partly because their creature-subjects are not dressed up as human beings. After Bishop had looked long and long at animals in their actual habitats, she let them 'show their relations' to her on their terms, not hers. 'Roosters', which lies somewhere between fable and moralised realism, remains one of her most arresting poems for this reason.

A single versified animal fable appears in the *Complete Poems*. It is called 'A Word with You' and is not, I think, a poem that Bishop herself would have chosen to republish. Written in 1933 when she was twenty-two and caught up in the *Con Spirito* controversy at Vassar, it lampoons lesser writers and critics from the point of view of a superior poet. In a zoo of literary pretenders, the speaker tries to have an intimate word with an artistic equal, but she can never reach the point of communicating because a crowd of animals is forever interrupting. Typically, Bishop's language is fresh and forceful, and she jumps right into her one-sided dialogue: 'Look out! there's that damned ape again . . . ' Advising her companion to sit still 'until he goes,/ or else forgets the things he knows,' the speaker suggests playing with rings to distract the creature. (Note the very Bishopian observation, 'Bright objects hypnotize the mind'.) With the ape temporarily *distrait*, the poets' talk resumes, only to be interrupted by the parrot, who alerts the monkeys, who take to squabbling over 'just one luscious adjective.' The question arises, how to control these infuriating inferiors who try to horn in on the poets' secrets? Some writers manage by treating them without feeling, throwing books at them or training them to bow. The speaker might 'keep order' in an authoritarian way, but she doesn't know how, especially given a most unpleasant cockatoo who 'can't bear any form of wit,' who might bite, and whom nothing escapes. The conferring poets fall into silence as, once more, 'the ape has overheard.'

When she wrote 'A Word with You', young élitist Miss Bishop may have had in mind exactly which girls at Vassar she intended the ape, the parrot and the cockatoo to represent. Taken more generally, the menagerie stands for a whole class of literary hangers-on that Bishop especially despised. Writing to me from Brazil in January 1964, she quoted Gibbon on the decay of letters in imperial Rome – acidly implying that in New York, the literary pundits of the twentieth-century had fallen to a comparable low: 'A cloud of critics, of compilers, of commentators, darkened the face of learning, and the decline of genius was soon followed by the corruption of taste.'[1] What she would have said today about criticism since 1979 doesn't bear thinking of. In view of her life-long scorn of most critics and almost all professional compilers and commentators, it is probably not surprising that through the chinks of her rumbustious little fable-satire, 'A Word with You', one never glimpses even a flicker of the tender, amused, animal-loving observer that shines through mature poems like 'Manners' and 'At the Fishhouses'. The animal-characters in 'A Word with You' are crude emblems of human types, never of nature's.

As is well known, a radical change in Bishop's poetry occurred once she had tuned her mind to the example of Marianne Moore. Almost at once, she put a stop to the baroque mannerisms she had affected at Vassar, as naturalness and 'completely accurate description' became the qualities she prized. In a tribute to Miss Moore published in 1948, Bishop even took it upon herself to criticise Shakespeare for grossly personifying a dying deer, comparing one of the more pastorally effusive passages in As You Like It unfavourably with Miss Moore's exact evocations of animal behaviour.[2] Curiously, as Bishop renounced the form of the moralising fable, it became attractive to Moore, whose animal-based didacticism increased as she grew older. In 1948, however, Bishop singled out for praise Moore's ability 'to give herself up entirely to the object under contemplation, to feel in all sincerity how it is to be it.' Being 'it' for Bishop meant knowing instinctively how not to confuse 'it' with herself. What is new and mysterious about 'The Fish' and 'The Moose' is the way the animals in their distinctness throw off the human world and by implication, judge it.

A question Bishop did not apparently put to herself, was how, exactly, she could make things and creatures 'think' without personifying them? In a number of early, experimental poems she was still impelled to rely on personifying devices. Take the somewhat surrealistic 'The Unbeliever', a poem she began working on in 1936. A man sleeps in a 'gilded ball' on top of a mast (notice that this is yet another poem about sleeping) 'with his eyes fast closed'; he wants to believe he won't fall, but can't. A cloud glides by and assures him that 'he', the cloud, is quite safe because he is built on marble pillars. Then a gull remarks that 'he', too, has nothing to worry about: the air is made of marble and will hold him up. The man alone, incapable of believing such untruths, is afraid to open his eyes to see what *is* true. The mast could be the tree of evolution, in which case man's position at the top of it is indeed precarious. With his eyes shut, the man tries to live in his dream – his blind faith? – which is 'I must not fall.' (I suppose one must take into account the theological implications of 'fall'.) The ironic title implies that nature believes in its permanence, however illusory, while man, foreseeing his end, tries to live in his dreams. Self-conscious, imaginative man is always, from nature's point of view, an 'unbeliever'.

Though the metaphysical cleverness of 'The Unbeliever' is not in question, one does worry about the speeches given to the cloud and gull. After all, if the poem is arguing that natural things cannot conceive of death while man's curse is that he has to, then it's pushing it a bit to have these natural things talk, or even 'believe', in a human sense. Moreover, the cloud and the gull themselves belong to different categories: one is a mere concentration of water vapour, the other is a living creature. Such considerations diminish the 'believability', if I can put it that way, of the cloud and gull, and in the end, the poem becomes not much more than a weird experiment.

About the time she was writing 'The Unbeliever', Bishop began a little prose piece called 'The Hanging of the Mouse' – a surprisingly shocking satire on the callousness and brutality of state punishment. Her idea came not from nature but from a toy mouse she had hung from a chair for her cat to play with; it may be that the poem occurred to her after she realised how really 'awful' it was to play at being natural in this way. Other fables she wrote after meeting Marianne Moore include 'The Sea & Its Shore' and 'In Prison' – sophisticated variations on ostensibly philosophical themes. These stories were similar to the parables she had published in *The Vassar Review* – one of which was called 'The Last Animal' – but they were her last in this line. Almost certainly, they reflect a perceived, stoic yet unanalysed uneasiness as they cast half-amused, half-terrified looks at her own strangeness. After 'In

Prison' won her a *Partisan Review* prize in 1938, she abandoned the mode altogether until nearly thirty years later, when her life was again in crisis in Brazil.

The *Complete Poems* oddly groups 'Rainy Season; SubTropics' – three prose-poems about Brazil's outsized creatures, 'Giant Toad', 'Strayed Crab' and 'Giant Snail' – with 'The Hanging of the Mouse' in a section of 'Uncollected Work', though the Brazilian pieces were written in the more personal vein Bishop adopted after she had been corresponding for some time with Robert Lowell. Neither fables, nor studies of nature, nor confessions, these untypical Brazilian pieces synthesise elements from all three literary genres, suggesting that however much Bishop intended to enter into the minds of and 'be' these creatures, she could not help creating them in something like her own image. When the Giant Toad tells us 'I am too big, too big by far. Pity me./ My eyes bulge and hurt . . . They see too much . . . ' we immediately connect its bigness and its too-much-seeing eyes with Bishop's own huge, handicapped talent. Bishop herself, no doubt, intended her toad to be more Darwinian than Mooresque – or Lowellesque – but her account of how some 'naughty children' made the snail smoke a cigarette is moralistic (how would a snail come by the word 'naughty'?) and the whole piece, like the others, is inconsequentially strange and sad. The Giant Snail's lament at the end of the triptych echoes the Toad's at the beinning: 'But O! I am too big. I feel it. Pity me.'

How different is the impression made by Bishop's classic, much-anthologized 'The Fish' in which a moral triumph is achieved precisely because the mind of the fisherpoet and the mind of the fish (if you can call it a mind) are held resolutely apart. In 'The Fish', Bishop's precepts about telling the truth in a poem, of letting 'what happened' guide its development, and particularly of looking 'long and long' at something until you are able to give yourself up 'entirely to the object under contemplation' are all wonderfully in evidence. Bishop herself wearied of seeing 'The Fish' anthologised, but its readers have not. In exact, natural yet unusual language, the poet's eyes explore the fish's every facet: his skin 'like ancient wallpaper' speckled with barnacles, his gills 'crisp with blood', his flesh 'packed in like feathers', his bones, entrails, and swim-bladder; then finally his eyes, emphatically not windows of the soul but 'more like the tipping / of an object toward the light.' The prolonged description draws to a climax when the poet observes 'five old pieces of fish-line,/ or four and a wire leader/ with the swivel still attached' hanging from the fish's lower 'lip'. The five ingrown hooks, like medals the fish has won in who knows what terrible wars of survival, ensure his 'victory'; which becomes even more, with the progressive revelation of the fish, a victory for the fisher-poet:

> I stared and stared
> And victory filled up
> the little rented boat,
> from the pool of bilge
> where oil had spread a rainbow
> around the rusted engine
> to the bailer rusted orange,
> the sun-cracked thwarts,
> the oarlocks on their strings,
> the gunnels – until everything
> was rainbow, rainbow, rainbow!
> And I let the fish go.

Like D. H. Lawrence in the final lines of 'The Snake', the writer at the end of 'The Fish' has exorcised 'a pettiness'. In a small way she has raised herself above nature by behaving humanly – that is, humanely, compassionately, empathetically. The rainbow is especially pertinent, both as a symbol of peace and unity – the rainbow that appeared to Noah after the flood – and as a prismatic breakdown of light into a natural array of colours. And yet Bishop has insured at the same time that we see it as an oil-rainbow in a pool of bilge. If her vision was Biblical (and also, of course,

Worthworthian) she kept her material modern. A reader, lost in admiration for the details – bailer, thwarts, gunnels, etc., not to mention the poet's control throughout of a natural-sounding three-stress line – is covertly warmed by the poem's 'moral' without noticing there is one.

A companion-piece to 'The Fish' is 'The Armadillo' written in Brazil twenty years later and published in *The New Yorker* in 1957. Once again, human beings and wild creatures confront each other in natural surroundings, but instead of concluding with a shared victory the poem ends with defeat. This defeat, though, does not, as one might expect, redound altogether to the shame of mankind; it's more as if Bishop were throwing up her hands in despair. June 24, or St John's Day, is the winter solstice in Brazil. In the 1950s (and probably still today) the superstitious locals lit (illegal) fire balloons and let them drift towards a saint's shrine in the mountains; if the balloons fell before the fire was extinguished, they set the forest burning. 'One's in two minds about them,' Bishop wrote to a friend in June 1955. While she liked the balloons' prettiness and the quaintness of the local custom, she was horrified at the havoc they wrought on the hill behind her house in Petrópolis.[3]

'The Armadillo' begins, then, in delight, describing the charm of the fire balloons, noting that their 'paper chambers' flush 'like hearts' and that the floating fires are hard to tell from the stars, or rather (with a typical Bishopian self-correction) the planets, and it proceeds with calm, meditative exactness until precisely midway through. At the end of the fifth stanza, the poet interrupts quietly with some alarming information: the balloons are dangerous. We are told how last night, one fell, splattering 'like an egg of fire', incinerating an owls' nest and driving out an armadillo, 'rose-flecked, head down, tail down'. When the armadillo was followed by a baby rabbit with short ears, soft as 'a handful of intangible ash', the poet herself began to see with 'fixed, ignited eyes' how the rabbit, the armadillo, and the owls had become helpless victims of a colourful superstition. The poem does not at first seem especially arresting. Its tone, established in three-and-four stress rhyming stanzas, tries to remain relaxed, colloquial, faithful to facts as always, so it is not until the last stanza that the poet's horror bursts out fully, in accusing italics:

> *Too pretty, dreamlike mimicry!*
> *O falling fire and piercing cry*
> *and panic, and a weak mailed fist*
> *clenched ignorant against the sky!*

The effectiveness of this outburst (it takes a while to see that it is effective) washes back over the stanzas that lead up to it, and a perceptive reader sees that the beautiful descriptions throughout were all along preparing for a tragic dénouement. 'Mimicry' suggests that the fire balloons, by appearing to sail between the 'sticks of the Southern Cross', illegitimately imitate stars and planets. A heaven that has been appropriated for religious purposes is no more identical with the 'real' cosmos than the 'weak mailed fist' of the armadillo is identical with an armed hand. The animals are 'ignorant' of ways to protect themselves against the predations of man, just as the superstitious Brazilians are blind to the natural laws common to themselves and the creatures. As in 'The Unbeliever', non-humans are victims of ignorance, humans are victims of blindness. In the end, no response is possible but that 'piercing cry' – a cry that is the natural response of human animals, too, when they are terrified.

Bishop's understanding of how humans and animals exist in separate spheres of ignorance and knowledge, and of where these spheres overlap and where they do not, was instinctive with her and not just a theory she picked up from reading Darwin. What she found in Charles Darwin was confirmation of her belief that the proper procedure for anyone who seeks knowledge is to begin by *looking* for it. To further her own excited explorations of an exotic topography resplendent with new flora and fauna, she had absorbed herself in *The Voyage of the Beagle* and probably *The Origin of Species* on first coming to Brazil. Like Darwin, she was determined to describe what she saw honestly and modestly, and if important truths could be 'pulled down from underneath' the natural material, so much the better. The so-called Darwin passage from her letter to me of 8 January 1964, famously examines her approach:

> I can't believe we are wholly irrational – and I do admire Darwin! But reading Darwin, one admires the beautiful solid case being built up out of his endless heroic *observations*, almost unconscious or automatic – and then comes a sudden relaxation, a forgetful phrase, and one feels the strangeness of his undertaking, sees the lonely young man, his eyes fixed on facts and minute detail, sinking or sliding giddily off into the unknown.

The phrase 'sliding giddily off into the unknown' may or may not rightly describe Darwin's wonder as he set about his naturalist investigations, but it certainly characterises Elizabeth Bishop's approach to her art. Bishop would not, probably, have been happy as a scientist, though she sometimes thought otherwise. Very likely, with Marianne Moore, she believed that the poet and scientist work 'analogously'. She certainly shared with Darwin (and Moore) a respect for the autonomy of the animals. Yet she was far too much an artist to repel, in the interest of scientific detachment, those precious, irrational glimpses of what she called in the same Darwin letter 'the surrealism of every day life'. The animals that appear in her later poems represent reassuring states of mind; they are significantly uninvestigated outsiders, like children and primitive people, whose simplicities sometimes offered her consolation, sometimes insight. In 'Five Flights Up' the bird waking on his branch, the little dog bounding cheerfully around a neighbour's yard, even the neighbour who scolds the dog, 'You ought to be ashamed!' provide evidence of an enviable world in which 'everything is answered,/ all taken care of,/ no need to ask again.' Once again, happiness, for Bishop, blesses such creatures as can take existence for granted without questioning it; while she herself – looking out from the top of her mast with her eyes wide open – more than often finds 'yesterday' (i.e. the past about which *she* cannot help feeling guilty) 'almost impossible to lift.' Animals in Bishop's poems, though they can signify other things, insist on being alive: the little dog in 'Five Flights Up', the hairless 'Pink Dog' trotting bravely through the streets of Rio, the cat that jumps into bed in 'Electrical Storm', even the goats in 'Crusoe in England'; we have to believe they somewhere 'really happened'. Loomingly real as any of them is the cow moose, however 'grand, otherworldly', that emerges from the 'impenetrable' New Brunswick wood towards the end of what, to me, is Elizabeth Bishop's wisest, most mysterious and spiritually profound poem, 'The Moose'.

Although Elizabeth Bishop did not finish writing 'The Moose' until June 1972, she had at least begun thinking about it twenty-six years earlier. A letter to Marianne Moore of 29 August 1946 mentions that during an all-night, really 'dreadful' bus trip from Great Village to Boston, 'just as it was getting light, the driver had to stop suddenly for a big cow moose who was wandering down the road. She walked away very slowly into the woods, looking at us over her shoulder. The driver said that one foggy night he had to stop while a huge bull moose came right up and smelled the engine. "Very curious beasts," he said.'[4] Such was the occasion that eventually generated twenty-eight stanzas of descriptive verse in which facts were only slightly altered to suit the requirements of a poem. At the same time, 'The Moose' is so much more than a description that the resonances it achieves suggest the truth of an insight offered in another of Bishop's letters: in some ways, she and Robert Lowell believed, they were both descended from the New England Transcendentalists.[5]

Most of 'The Moose' takes place in one or the other of two mental landscapes. In a typical Bishopian fashion, the first opens our eyes to the 'real' scenery or geography through which the bus passes, while the second sets our minds free to drift off into a dreamy state half-way between consciousness and unconsciousness. The scenery described is an exact evocation of the Minas Basin around the Bay of Fundy. We are told about the 'long tides' and the red soil and the river's 'wall of brown foam.' We are shown the fog settling into beds of sweet peas and cabbages; we say goodbye to the sugar maples, the elms, the clapboard churches and farmhouses. It is still possible to take 'the moose route' from Great Village along the coast, past Bass River, Lower, Middle and Upper Economy, Five Islands (spectacular lumps of red sandstone), Five Houses and then up across the Cobequid hills and Chignecto Bay into New Brunswick. In Bishop's poem, however, once we have got the geography under our eyes, we are drawn away from it, as night falls, into an eternity of memories. As the bus enters the 'hairy, scratchy, splintery' moonlit woods, 'somewhere,/ back in the bus' the passengers begin their 'dreamy divagations'. And who are these half-ghosts talking as if under enchantment, rehearsing their small, sad, significant lives as they pass into the past as naturally as they once settled to sleep 'in the old feather-bed'?

> Grandparents' voices
>
> uninterruptedly
> talking in Eternity:
> names being mentioned,
> things cleared up finally;
> what he said, what she said,
> who got pensioned;
>
> deaths, deaths and sicknesses;
> the year he remarried;
> the year (something) happened.
> She died in childbirth.

> That was the son lost
> when the schooner foundered.
>
> He took to drink. Yes.
> She went to the bad.
> When Amos began to pray
> even in the store and
> finally the family had
> to put him away.

When suddenly the moose appears, disrupting this stream of memories (all of which, notice, relate to Elizabeth Bishop's own story) the driver jolts the passengers awake, putting on his brakes. By this time, both they and we, as readers, are prepared for something 'otherwordly' to happen. And in fact, *it does happen*; the moose *does* appear from another world, though the revelation, far from being supernatural, is just the reverse. The moose becomes the *natural* focus of the passengers' ephemeral, dream-like wanderings:

> Taking her time,
> she looks the bus over,
> grand, otherworldly.
> Why, why do we feel
> (we all feel) this sweet
> sensation of joy?

Reminding us of her Brazilian poem, 'The Riverman', Bishop suggests in 'The Moose' that the only believable alternative world has to be a natural world which teaches us how to accept and be reconciled to the creatures we are. 'Look, it stands to reason,' says the Amazonian Indian who aspires to become a *sacaca* in 'The Riverman', 'that everything we need comes from the river . . . one just has to know how to find it.' The implication is that for those who are *called*, for those with patience to *learn how to see*, the river (of life and ourselves within it) is all we have of magic, and all we need. Transcendent knowledge is a knowledge of nature that transcends us. The moose, like the Dolphin and Luandinha in 'The Riverman', 'calls' to everyone on the bus, but it's the poet who answers for them, committing herself to twenty-five years' study to get the magic right.

The large time-gap between 1946, when 'The Moose' was conceived, and June 1972, when Bishop read the poem at a Phi Beta Kappa ceremony at Harvard, is a measure of how long it took for the moose's reality to become emblematic in a way that would satisfy the demands the poet came to make of her craft. One never wants to make too much of terminology, but it may be worth suggesting that in 'The Moose' Elizabeth Bishop, in her instinctive way, was reaching back for the very earliest form in which people conceded power to the animals they at once feared and exploited, revered and depended upon. Behind the civilized, creature-diminishing conventions of the fable lie thousands of years of primitive *totemic* art, tribal acknowledgement by imitation or depiction of the beasts' intrinsic importance to human societies.

The word 'totem', as defined by the Oxford English Dictionary, originated with the North American Indians for whom the 'otem' (in Nova Scotia's Acadia, 'aoutem') signifies, usually, an animal ancestor with which a tribe identifies and from which its members consider themselves to be descended. Anthropologists have extended 'totemism' to include the mythopoeic beliefs of the Australian aborigines. And indeed, if we broaden our reach to include the animal superstitions of the ancient Mediterranean peoples, the haruspications of the Greeks and Romans, the animal-deities of the Egyptians and Africans and the internment of horses and dogs with the dead in almost all ancient cultures; if we further call to mind the unknown Europeans who painted the caves at Lascaux, or remember that medieval warriors appropriated images of wild beasts for heraldic purposes; and if we consider that even the anthropocentric first Christians found an emblem for their Saviour in the figure of a fish, later coming to represent their chief apostles by an ox, a lion, and an eagle, we can begin to see, even without recourse to modern anthropological scholarship, how throughout history our human ideas of self and society have sought reassurance by connecting us mystically or practically with other live creatures with whom we share the planet.

In suggesting that the moose in Elizabeth Bishop's poem attains, towards the end, something of totemic status, I don't want to push too far in the direction of anthropology. At the same time, its sudden appearance does make what we might call a 'tribe' out of the passengers on the bus. All of them are stirred, moved, drawn out of themselves by something natural and inspiriting to which they know they belong:

> Why, why do we feel
> (we all feel) this sweet
> sensation of joy?

Though it took Elizabeth Bishop a long time to answer the call of 'The Moose', she apparently had worked out its loosely rhymed six-line, three-stress stanza form by the fall of 1956, when, writing from Brazil, she told her aunt Grace Bowers in Nova Scotia that she would dedicate a long poem to her when it was finished.[6] To set down 'what really happened' in personal letters must have been easy for her, or comparatively easy, while crystalising these same impressions in poems required years of patience and concentration. In some cases, the discipline of a set form seems to have helped. By selecting a fairly rigid stanza pattern for 'The Moose' she ensured that she could not get away with finishing it too soon. The looser unrhymed lines of 'The Riverman' gave her more freedom, but then 'The Riverman' was one of a few poems she based on her reading (in this case, Charles Wagley's *Amazon Town*) rather than on her own experience.

For whatever reason, Elizabeth Bishop chose to keep 'The Moose' flowing through regular stanzas, and in this respect it resembles an earlier long poem, 'Roosters', which dates from her Key West days and was first published in 1940 (only six years, after all, before she began meditating on 'The Moose'). For 'Roosters' Bishop borrowed a three-line stanza from one of her seventeenth-century favourites, Richard Crashaw. Since Crashaw's 'To His (Supposed) Mistress' has nothing in common with 'Roosters' but its verse-pattern, it may be that Bishop had tried and failed to use the form during her baroque period at Vassar. Here are Crashaw's (very famous) opening lines:

> Who ere she bee,
> That not impossible shee
> That shall comand my heart and mee;
>
> Where ere shee lye,
> Lock't up from mortall Eye,
> In shady leaves of Destiny . . .

And here is the beginning of 'Roosters':

> At four o'clock
> in the gun-metal blue dark
> we hear the first crow of the first cock
>
> just below
> the gun-metal blue window
> and immediatedly there is an echo . . .

Elizabeth Bishop thought of 'Roosters' as her war poem, though like her depression poem, 'A Miracle for Breakfast', it is hardly the kind of political writing we are used to today. When in October 1940 Marianne Moore and her mother criticized 'Roosters' for its 'vulgarities', naïvely sending her a rewritten version of their own entitled 'The Cock', Bishop protested that she cherished 'sordidities' such as 'water-closet' and 'dropping-plastered hen-house floor' because she wanted to emphasise 'the essential baseness of militarism.' The Moores, horrified at Bishop's 'vio-lence', transformed Bishop's tin rooster into a gold one and, completely missing the form's implicit bow to Crashaw, innocently chopped lines out of the stanzas they disapproved of.* Miss Moore's misappropriation of 'Roosters' virtually brought to an end the relationship of dependence Bishop had developed with her poetic 'mother' over six and more years. Though she did not entirely stop sending Moore drafts of new poems, Bishop never again quite trusted her to understand the direction in which she was moving. As Kalstone demonstrates, after Bishop had published *North & South* and in consequence met Robert Lowell, Lowell became her chief confident and critic, while Marianne Moore, beloved as she was, faded somewhat into the background.

The Moores' criticism, however, did persuade Bishop to go over 'Roosters' again, causing her to remove capital letters from the beginnings of lines and to reconsider, maybe, just what it was that made the poem important to her. It must have been obvious even in 1941, when 'Roosters' appeared in a supplement to *The New Republic*, that here was yet another poem set at dawn, in that borderland between sleeping and waking where so many Bishop poems take place. 'Love Lies Sleeping', 'Paris, 7 A.M.', and 'Sleeping Standing Up' all conclude with a struggle between consciousness and unconsciousness. In the last of these, consciousness wins, driving out 'the armored cars of dreams' into a limbo of unknowing; in the first, it looks as if insensibility (or death) has 'revealed' something important through its distortion. In 'Roosters', by contrast, the emphasis falls entirely on what is happening *outside* the sleeper's mind, each rooster screaming, 'This is where I live!'/ Each screaming / 'Get up! Stop dreaming!'" And though here, just as in 'The Moose', an outside happening *naturally* intrudes into a dream-state, the 'dreadful' roosters – at least throughout the first part of the poem – represent the reverse of the moose's wonderful revelation.

* The Moores' version has been preserved in the Marianne Moore archive at Bryn Mawr and is to be found in an appendix to David Kalstone's *Becoming a Poet*.

Where the moose preserves its mooseness from the moment it enters its poem, Bishop's roosters suggest something else (though, of course, they are real, too). The epithet 'gun-metal' twice repeated, gives us our clue, and as Bishop herself pointed out to Marianne Moore, the enumerated 'sordidities' were always *meant* to condemn the 'baseness of militarism'. The noise, stupidity and vulgar display of the be-medalled roosters, with their macho contempt for those unfortunate 'wives' and the air-battles to the death they fight among themselves, do seem to be, in the terminology I have been using, as much fabulistic as naturalistic. In working out the overall pattern of 'Roosters', Bishop unconsciously managed to combine several genres. The birds are first of all really roosters whose crowings wake the speaker up; secondly, their war-like appearance and behaviour suggest a fable in the mould of Chaucer's tale of Chauntecleer and Pertolete. And thirdly, in the middle section of the poem, with the introduction of references to St Peter and Mary Magdalen, it becomes evident that 'Roosters' has moved into the 'heraldic' or symbolic framework of the Christian story.

If we divide the poem into three parts, then, Part I ends with the contemptuous, almost amused stanza in which a rooster-warrior fallen in battle is flung on the dung heap 'with his dead wives/ with open, bloody eyes,/ while those metallic feathers oxidize' (stanza twenty-six). Part II consists of thirteen stanzas relating to St Peter's denial of Christ, a story that medieval and Renaissance artists preserved in church sculpture ('explained by *gallus canit;/flet Petrus* underneath it') and that still ornaments weathervanes 'on basilica and barn'. These thirteen stanzas compose the moral heart of the poem ('There is inescapable hope, the pivot') and they redeem, really, the sins of war committed at the beginning. The five stanzas of Part III, which acts as a sort of coda to the main action, draw together all the poem's themes in images at once conciliatory and ambiguous. The scene shifts to morning in Key West where 'a low light is floating/ in the back yard and gilding/ from underneath/

the broccoli, leaf by leaf . . . '. Fully awake now, the poet asks her accustomed question, 'how could the night have come to grief?'. We are back, apparently, in the predicament stated at the end of 'Sleeping Standing Up': 'How stupidly we steered/ until the night was past/ and never found out where the cottage was.' Except that this time the day's 'preamble' is a natural revelation 'like wandering lines in marble.' As morning arrives, the cocks become 'almost inaudible'; they are embodiments of evils now almost forgotten. And like St Peter on the night of Christ's betrayal, the rising sun follows 'to see the end' (see *The Gospel According to St Matthew* 26:58). In one of the finest last lines in twentieth-century poetry, Bishop expresses the ambivalent significance of the roosters and St Peter in one levelling, wide-open, disturbingly truthful phrase: 'faithful as enemy, or friend.'

The rising sun at the end of 'Roosters' anticipates the motif of an extraordinary poem with which Bishop chose to end *North & South*. 'Anaphora', which in the terminology of rhetoric means repetition, begins more or less where 'Roosters' left off, with a morning already 'white-gold' with heat as the sleeper wakes to the sound of birds and bells and factory whistles. The question asked is not, this time, 'how could the night have come to grief?' but 'Where is the music coming from, the energy?'. Such a day must have been meant for some 'ineffable creature' – the god Helios? Apollo? Christ? – whom we must have missed, and always do miss. For as soon as we rise 'he/ appears and takes his earthly nature', condemning himself to fall 'victim' of human intrigue, memory 'and mortal/ mortal fatigue.' The second stanza traces the decline of this god-like creature through the gradual exhaustion of every day's 'drift of bodies' (a defeat of dreams, of the imagination) to his guttering as a 'beggar in the park', who nevertheless and despite his degradation prepares new dreams and more searching 'stupendous studies' for the sun's 'fiery event/ of every day in endless/ endless assent.' The word *assent* – indicating an acceptance, however reluctant, of the dialectic that imagination forever carries on with mortality – immediately brings to mind its homophone, *ascent*. The implication is that with the sun's assent/ascent, every day begins with an epiphany that instantly disintegrates; that every night ends with a resurrection of imagination's (mortal) energy.

It seems pretty clear that when Elizabeth Bishop put together *North & South*, she thought of it as ascending from the aesthetic geography of 'The Map' through the quasi-surrealism of 'The Man-Moth' and 'The Weed' through the natural mediations of 'The Fish' and 'Roosters' to the death and resurrection of imagination implied in 'Anaphora'. Planning her other books thematically must also have been an objective, which suggests that the finical, surprisingly small corpus of her work composes in itself something of an anaphora. Motifs and ideas expressed in one book are repeated, with variations, in others. The drift of her work runs generally from the abstract to the concrete, from metaphysical speculation on the nature of dream-experience and art to later, concrete evocations of her personal life – though, of course, this development was not logically arrived at. Her letters to Marianne Moore and Robert Lowell continually accuse herself of laziness or complain of her inability to write a more popular or else a more 'serious' kind of poetry. No doubt she did feel blocked and helpless much of the time. As an artist, though, she knew instinctively and better than any critic what she could do in writing, and what she couldn't. One of the things she could do best was write metaphorically, even symbolically, without appearing to do so. What is most fascinating about the role of animals and birds in her poetry is their ambivalent status both as natural creatures and, as we have seen, various types of emblem.

It seems, therefore, appropriate to end this chapter with some remarks about 'Sandpiper' – a 'creature poem' in which the poet herself seems to be, in I. A. Richard's critical terms, the 'tenor' in a metaphor for which the bird is an unwitting 'vehicle'. 'Sandpiper' was doubtless begun after Bishop had observed an actual sandpiper running in and out of the surf on a North Atlantic beach.

Already in the first stanza, however, the sandpiper is established as a 'he', the personal pronoun Elizabeth Bishop usually chose when writing obliquely of herself:

> The roaring alongside he takes for granted,
> and that every so often the world is bound to shake.
> He runs, he runs to the south, finical, awkward,
> in a state of controlled panic, a student of Blake.

References to the south and to Blake point the poem very plainly in a personal direction, though it is not as self-pitying as the prose of 'Rainy Season: Sub Tropics'. Everything the sandpiper sees or does reminds us of the poet: the shaking world and hissing beach, the sheets of terrifying water through which he runs 'watching his toes' (correction, 'Watching, rather, the spaces of sand between them'), the details (none too small) of his focussed obsession, the mist which clears momentarily to reveal a world 'minute and vast and clear'. What language could more exactly represent Bishop's preoccupation with 'looking for something, something, something'? In the last two lines, the sandpiper is lost sight of – maybe he's run off down the beach in a blur of obsessive activity – as the poet, despairing of finding a final, 'all-out' answer to implied questions of why and where and how, fixes her gaze on the sand:

> The millions of grains are black, white, tan, and grey,
> mixed with quartz grains, rose and amethyst.

CHAPTER FOUR

The Geographical Mirror

There is grandeur in this view of life, with its several powers,
having been originally breathed into a few forms or into one; and
that whilst this planet has gone cycling on according to the fixed
law of gravity, from so simple a beginning endless forms most
beautiful and most wonderful have been and are being evolved.

Charles Darwin, *The Origin of Species* (1859)

It is like what we imagine knowledge to be:
dark, salt, clear, moving, utterly free.

'At the Fishhouses'

In June of 1935, when Elizabeth Bishop and a Vassar friend, Harriet
Tomkins, set off for Europe in the Nazi ship S.S. *Königstein*, Adolf
Hitler had been in power for over two years. Harriet Tomkins
recalled that as their boat pulled out of New York, a mass of Nazi
sympathizers stood on the dock raising their arms in the Hitler
salute. 'Oh, how horrible. It's like the dead,' cried Elizabeth, who
came to detest the too 'earthy' Germans who trampled over her
during the voyage.[1] Yet after the unpleasantness of the crossing, the
girls saw nothing in the Low Countries and France but what
delighted them. Like many young Americans of the time, they
tended to look upon Europe as a vast museum, a continent richly
provided with artistic achievements indispensable to the continu-
ation of their private educations. Between the New World and the
Old, between Henry James's brash, ignorant America and corrupt,

artstuffed Europe, lay the wide Atlantic, protecting American travellers with thick layers of isolationist blindfold.

World War II, when it came, profoundly affected Elizabeth Bishop, who by then had found a home in Key West, Florida. Yet the war, which brought the US Navy to Key West, makes only a tangential appearance in her 1946 collection, North & South. So little attention did her poems give to it that when her first book was published Bishop insisted on offering her readers an apology. In a letter of 22 January 1945 to Ferris Greenslet, literary advisor to Houghton Mifflin, she wrote: 'The fact that none of these poems deal directly with the war, at a time when so much war poetry is being published, will, I am afraid, leave me open to reproach. The chief reason is simply that I work very slowly. But I think it would help some if a note to the effect that most of the poems had been written, or begun at least, before 1941, could be inserted at the beginning say, just after the acknowledgments.'[2]

The note duly appeared, though the book's publication was delayed for more than a year and a half. It came out at last on August 20, 1946, when Elizabeth for the first time in many years was visiting friends and family in Nova Scotia. By that time the war was history. Five years later, a number of literary awards helped the poet to escape from the Eastern seaboard of North America and start a new life in Brazil. Yet it was not until several years after that, when she was settled with Lota de Macedo Soares in Petrópolis, that Elizabeth Bishop, on the advice of her publishers, brought out a reprint of North & South with the addition of twenty new poems she had completed for a second collection, A Cold Spring. It was this second book, published by Houghton Mifflin in July 1955, that won her the Pulitzer Prize in 1956 and, later that year, a Partisan Review Fellowship of twenty-seven hundred dollars.

All this time, Bishop was worried about her poetry's lack of social consciousness, fearing she would be condemned as insufficiently serious. 'Roosters', indeed, she defended as a war poem, though, as we have seen, midway through it shifts into the wider moral perspectives of New Testament iconography before ending in an ambiguous coda. Likewise, Part III of 'Songs for a Colored Singer' looks at the war only dreamily to dismiss it:

> Lullaby.
> Sleep on and on,
> war's over soon.
> Drop the silly, harmless toy,
> pick up the moon.

No doubt Bishop felt the pressure of contemporary events and wished to write about them, yet her active imagination, while it responded angrily to perceived acts of cruelty or inhumanity, was too interrogatory and, above all, too reflective to feel comfortable with polemical arguments. At Vassar, she had concerned herself unwillingly with politics. As she grew older, a resigned realism bordering on fatalism led her to despair of the human condition. 'My outlook is pessimistic,' she wrote in January 1964. 'I think we are still barbarians, barbarians who commit a hundred indecencies and cruelties every day of our lives . . . but I think we should be gay in spite of it, sometimes even giddy, – to make life endurable and to keep ourselves "new, tender, quick." '[3] In her poetry, though not always in her life, Elizabeth Bishop did her best to be 'gay in spite of it'. Sometimes she played the child: 'Drop the silly, harmless toy.' Sometimes, as in the witty 'Cirque d'Hiver', she allowed herself to become gently sceptical of progress: 'Well, we have come this far.' But most often she tried to show that in hopeless human situations *something* can be salvaged; something can be found, usually in the minutiae of a landscape or in the heartwarming, sympathetic details of a domestic scene, to make life, in George Herbert's words, 'new, tender, quick.'[4]

*   *   *

In 1955, *Poems: North & South – A Cold Spring* came out in one slim volume and was reviewed as a single book. Yet it represents twenty years of Bishop's fastidious self-revision and consists, really, of three books, or three distinct parts.

In the first part – set in the North of *North & South* – twenty poems consider, from various angles, the nature of imagination. They relate to Bishop's outlook (and inlook) as a young writer in New York and as a traveller to 1930s Paris. As we have seen, many of these take place in a twilight zone between sleeping and waking, and Bishop would have agreed that their mood and general ambiance are surrealistic.* The poems of the second section are for the most part set in Florida – the title's South – eight out of ten of them deftly catching the look and 'feel' of that state. Their unstated, unifying preoccupation, however, has subtly to do with vulnerability, with the apparent contingency of humankind to the natural world. In the third section, intended to be a separate book called *A Cold Spring*, Bishop broods over and explores ideas introduced in the first two, moving away from 'The Map' and its map-makers' aesthetic into the more literal, personal geographies of 'A Cold Spring', 'Over 2,000 Illustrations and a Complete Concordance', 'The Bight', 'At the Fishhouses' and 'Cape Breton'. These wonderfully realised meditations do indeed hold up a mirror to nature, yet (and this, I think, is why the poems are so hypnotic) the mind that speculates and reflects in them also terribly desires to be reflected. The phrase 'the geographical mirror' was one Bishop noted down while visiting the coast of Nova Scotia in the summer of 1946, a time when she was consciously attempting, says Brett Millier, to find 'knowledge' and a meaning for herself in that rocky, ice-cold landscape she associated with her mother.[5] But before looking at Bishop's interior reflections and debates in *A*

---

* By 1964, Bishop had abandoned the surrealist model and was proposing as an alternative 'The always-more-successful surrealism of everyday life.' (Letter, 8 January 1964.)

Cold Spring and its successor, *Questions of Travel*, it will be helpful
to consider what she had achieved and was achieving in the poems
set in Key West.

Elizabeth Bishop, with Louise Crane, first visited Florida in the
winter of 1936–7, after returning from their first trip to Europe.
From a fishing resort called the Keewayden Club, Elizabeth was
soon sending excited letters back to New Yorkbound Marianne
Moore, describing the rich, natural 'fantasy' of the landscape and
exulting in a new friendship with 'a sort of Tarzan' named Charles
(Red) Russell and his wife, Charlotte (Sha-Sha). The Russells,
neither one of whom was literary, introduced her to Ross Allen,
famous for public exhibitions of snake-handling and alligator-
wrestling. It was Ross Allen who, on a memorable occasion in the
back of the Russells' car, taught Bishop the five calls of the
alligator.[6] Later she sailed with Louise to the tip of the Florida
Keys and fell in love with Key West. When Louise returned to New
York in mid-January, Elizabeth stayed on at the Keewayden Club
with the Russells, fishing and drafting a poem she later called
'Florida'.

The poem represented a new departure for her, although it owes
as much to Marianne Moore's poetics as it does to Ross Allen's
expertise in shells and alligators. It is interesting to observe how
Bishop borrowed Moore's tapestried style while disregarding her
experimental forms and her moralising purposes. While the em-
broidered vocabulary of 'Florida' could be mistaken for Moore's –
in, for example, Moore's poem 'Virginia Britannia' – Bishop allows
her lines a good deal more lyrical freedom. And while, like Moore,
she insists on being *present* in her poem, she eschews shaping it into
a homily. All in all, 'Virginia Britannia' is a denser and perhaps more
satisfactory piece of visual evocation than 'Florida', yet a compari-
son of their conclusions brings out important differences. The last
stanza of 'Virginia Britannia' reads:

The live oak's darkening filigree
of undulating boughs, the etched
solidity of a cypress indivisible
from the now aged English hackberry,
become with lost identity,
part of the ground, as sunset flames increasingly
against the leaf-chiseled
blackening ridge of green; while clouds, expanding above
the town's assertiveness, dwarf it, dwarf arrogance
that can misunderstand
importance; and
are to the child an intimation of what glory is.

Night arrives, too, at the end of 'Florida', but Bishop has nothing
obvious to say about assertiveness or arrogance:

Cold white, not bright, the moonlight is coarse-meshed,
and the careless, corrupt state is all black specks
too far apart, and ugly whites; the poorest
post-card of itself.
After dark, the pools seem to have slipped away.
The alligator, who has five distinct calls:
friendliness, love, mating, war, and a warning
whimpers and speaks in the throat
of the Indian Princess.

While both poems lay emphasis on natural events in such a way
as to show that loss of identity can only advance perception,
Marianne Moore slips in a criticism of (human) arrogance at the
end, where Bishop leaves the last word to the alligator, guiding her
reader's mind back to that imaginary, despoiled Indian Princess
whose 'skirt' (the Florida coastline) she has already described as
ornamented with strings of faded shells 'arranged as on a gray rag
of rotted calico'.

Bishop's instinct was to look hard enough at nature to lose

herself in it – and thus, as in the Biblical paradox, find herself. Marianne Moore, for all her modernism, was proud to include herself in a long line of literary moralists. She took pains to divert her essentially bookish accumulation of knowledge into the production of right thinking poetic essays. Her ostrich in 'He "Digesteth Harde Yron" ', for example, is identified in the first stanza as the 'camel-sparrow' chosen by Xenophon as 'a symbol of justice.' In the same vain, she begins 'The Buffalo' by informing her readers that 'Black in blazonry means/ prudence; and nigger, unpropitious' before going on to speculate, 'Might/ hematite-/ black, compactly incurved horns on bison/ have significance?'. The beasts and birds have never, surely, attracted a more literary observer. Still, Moore's sharp, educated eye would not argue with her indignant defence of natural propriety. Even in a light poem describing three fledgling mocking birds stalked by a cat, she could not bring herself to let the cat kill one; instead the mother bird heroically 'wages deadly combat' and then improbably wounds the 'intellectual cautious-/ly creeping cat.'

When she met Moore in March 1934, Elizabeth Bishop approached the older poet's work cautiously. Later, she put herself to school with Moore and learned – or taught herself – how to manipulate the mirror of her own mind. At the same time, Moore, for all her literary boldness, was ill-equipped for a life of Darwinian struggle. Settled – despite rash expeditions to the zoo and the baseball diamond – in almost hypochondriac seclusion with her mother in Brooklyn, she shaped her fables around creatures amenable to her imagination. As Randall Jarrell once slyly remarked, she sent her postcards only to the nicer animals. Bishop, on the other hand, found mental relief in physical activity, and she was drawn to Florida at first for the fishing. More importantly, by the time Elizabeth Bishop met her, Marianne Moore was fiercely set in her opinions. Bishop, conversely, approached the unknown like a tantalizing, perpetually elusive creative territory; imaginatively, she wanted to live nowhere else. It is hardly possible, therefore, to conceive of Bishop 'taking possession' of nature, as David Kalstone observed Moore doing time and time again. In Bishop's view, nature, to use Kalstone's words, was more likely 'to reclaim the world for itself, assert its own economy . . . miming our need for comfort but [continuing] utterly heedless of us.'[7]

Bishop's first visit to Florida in the winter of 1936–7 was a matter of a few weeks' fishing, but after a second trip to Europe the following summer (the summer of the car accident in France) she and Louise Crane decided to buy a house (624 White Street) in Key West. At the time, Key West was a semi-paradisaical, quasi-colonial settlement inhabited by an assortment of artists, writers, retired people, hangers-on and alcoholics who mixed cheerfully with an easy-going Cuban population that immediately won Bishop's heart. Writing to Marianne Moore in January 1938, Bishop took pleasure in describing the tiny houses with scrolls like paper cutouts, whose huge flowering plants seemed to have 'sapped the strength of everything else in town.' She was especially taken with 'a very small cottage' down the street from her (then) boarding house. 'The only furniture [the cottage] contains,' she went on, 'besides a bed and chair is an enormous French horn, painted silver, leaning against the wall, and hanging over it a pith helmet, also painted silver.'[8] The description found its way into the enchanting stanzas of 'Jerónimo's House', one in a group of Key West poems that take for a subject the endearing frailty of people who live on the margins of existence:

> My house, my fairy
>   palace, is
> of perishable
>   clapboards with
> three rooms in all,
>   my grey wasps' nest
> of chewed-up paper
>   glued with spit.

Such an arrangement of short, tentative lines, each one a brush stroke in a word-painting, ensures that we all but walk into Jerónimo's front room, festive with left-over Christmas decorations, noting the blue wicker table and chairs, a fried fish on the table 'spattered with burning scarlet sauce'; a French horn, painted silver, hung on a hook; the night radio playing flamencos, and so on. Towards the end it begins to be clear that the subject of the poem is the speaker-owner of all these beautiful things, one of the meek who has inherited all he needs of the earth by dint of not raising himself very far above it. Though his position is precarious, it is touchingly satisfactory:

> When I move
> I take these things,
>   not much more, from
> my shelter from
>   the hurricane.

What Jerónimo cannot see, though the poet can, is that a war beyond his child-like horizon will bring in the US Navy to root up his shelter as efficiently as any hurricane; or if not that, his sense of security, of belonging so beautifully to his place, will be swept away as civilization 'advances'. Bishop, even as she mimes Jerónimo's soft-speaking voice, fears that his innocence is doomed. She doesn't say so, of course, but the very existence of her inventory suggests that nothing in Jerónimo's house can survive for very long.

Others among these poems set in Key West are less freighted with invisible wistfulness, giving attention instead to the island's dramatic (then not so spoiled) scenery. All of them subliminally pass judgement on conceit and self-importance. 'Seascape' wryly makes fun of opposing Christian theologies, pitting angel-like Renaissance herons in their mangrove heaven against a puritanical lighthouse 'in black and white clerical dress' who thinks that 'hell rages below his iron feet' and who, when it gets dark, 'will remember something/ strongly worded to say on the subject.'

'Little Exercise' – an exercise in visual imagination – describes the hot coast rejoicing in the freshness and wetness of a Florida thunderstorm. At the end, the tiny figure of 'someone sleeping in the bottom of a row-boat' (one of Bishop's humans who are 'blind' to nature's dangers) lies unaware of the dramatic 'battle-scenes' being enacted around him. The poem instructs us to think of such a figure reassuringly, as 'uninjured, barely disturbed' – which places him in a more advantageous position than the black servant in 'Cootchie', drowned (one assumes) and lying irretrievably 'below the surface of the coral-reef'. Cootchie, we know from Bishop's letters, was a real person (as Miss Lula was, and 'Jerónimo', too). Cootchie's death has deprived Miss Lula of a servant not much more underprivileged than herself, though social distinctions between mistress and maid had been preserved when Cootchie ate 'her dinner off the kitchen sink/while Lula ate hers off the kitchen table.' The poignancy of this little domestic scene is brought about not so much by two lonely women's show of racial and social propriety as by the sad futility of their interdependence:

> Tonight the moonlight will alleviate
> the melting of the pink wax roses
>   planted in tin cans filled with sand
> placed in a line to mark Miss Lula's losses;
>   but who will shout and make her understand?
> Searching the land and sea for someone else,
> the lighthouse will discover Cootchie's grave
> and dismiss all as trivial; the sea, desperate,
>   will proffer wave after wave.

One can see why Marianne Moore would have disliked 'Cootchie', a poem that in its sympathy and simplicity, offers no moral or religious consolation whatsoever. The puritanical lighthouse that found hell raging below *his* feet in 'Seascape' ceases to be comical when *it* dimisses 'all as trivial'; and the waves can only proffer themselves.

'Cootchie' (which, for the economy of its form, is a poem I especially admire) anticipates the more ambiguous relationship between a white mistress and a black servant explored in 'Faustina, or Rock Roses'. Bishop's letters show her toiling over 'Faustina' for six years, beginning it in Key West in December 1943, and completing it in 1948 or early '49, about the same time as 'Cape Breton', 'Over 2000 Illustrations and a Complete Concordance' and 'The Bight'. All these poems of the late '40s suggest that Bishop was writing at her best in this personally dark, self-accusing period of her life.

'Faustina' resembles 'Jerónimo's House' in that it behaves like a painting and ends in meaningful ambivalence. The canvas – a comparatively large one this time – shows three women in a 'crazy' sagging room, which, like the women themselves, is 'betrayed' (a pivotal and terrible word) by a naked eighty-watt bulb hanging from the ceiling. In the centre of the picture, a frail, dying old lady, painted entirely in sickly whites, lies helpless on a 'crazy' bed of chipped enamel. Over her head, the bed's 'four vaguely roselike/ flower-formations' introduce the rose motif that is so important in the poem. Less conspicuous is the neutral figure of a visitor (obviously the poet) who has brought the sick woman a bouquet, also of roses – and these, like the bed's enamel roses, must be seen as freckled dark and white. The third woman, approaching the bed 'on bare scraping feet', is the black servant, Faustina, who in exhibiting an array of arsenic-coloured items – talcum powder, pills, cans of 'cream', white bowl of farina – is the most powerful, most ambiguous figure in the painting. As black Faustina bends over her helpless white employer's white hair, white undershirt showing under the night-gown, white disordered sheets 'like wilted roses', the action freezes. The visitor perceives that Faustina's 'sinister kind face/ presents a cruel black/ coincident conundrum.' What does it mean – this Negro woman's 'sinister kind', 'cruel black' expression? 'Is it/ freedom at last, a lifelong/ dream of time and silence,/ . . . of protection and rest?/ Or is it the very worst,/ the unimaginable nightmare/ that never before dared last/ more than a second?'

The question 'forks instantly', presenting several sets of opposites. Does Faustina love and depend upon the protection of her mistress, or has she for a long time feared and hated her? When her mistress dies, will Faustina inherit enough to retire on, or will she be left penniless, without a job? Given her power to prolong her mistress's life or hasten her death, which will Faustina choose to do? To the observant visitor, 'The eyes say only either.' Mistress and servant are apparently caught in a frightening dilemma, racial and social. Nor does it seem that anything is resolved once the visitor rises, proffering 'her bunch/ of rust-perforated roses' – roses in which white and coloured pigments have 'rusted' inseparably into each other. As the visitor leaves, she despairs of answering her 'conundrum', transferring it instead to the flowers: 'oh, whence come all the petals.' How, in other words, do human relationships, like petals, come about? What are the evolutionary forces that have brought about this situation of suspect communication and worrying mistrust?

'Faustina', then, is a poem about race relations in the way 'Roosters' is a poem about war. Both, on one level, adopt a right-thinking, democratically approved attitude; yet in doing so they slip so far out of the noose of the expected that they create as many questions as they answer. Bishop's reach in 'Faustina, or Rock Roses' is both wider and narrower than the abstract problem it addresses; wider because, at the end, it takes the 'race question' out of the hands of society, putting it (and the culture that created it) in the much larger perspective of natural evolution; narrower because it focusses on one scene and three actors only.

There can be little doubt that the events described in 'Faustina' – including the visitor's ambivalent response – really happened. Elizabeth Bishop must literally have experienced that ambivalence, however much in minor ways she revised her experience, writing the poem. Then, too, 'Faustina' proceeds exactly in accordance with Bishop's rules for creating baroque art: her mind *thinks* the drama as it happens, reporting in the present tense. For although the poem resembles a painting, surely it is a painting-in-process, being created before our eyes. Look at the poet brushing in a detail: 'The visitor sits and watches/ the dew glint on the screen/ and in it two glow-worms/ burning a drowned green.' In executing the details of the first two stanzas, the artist has confined herself to different shades of white, but at this point she drops her white brush and picks up another, purposefully daubing in 'a drowned green'. Returning briefly to her white palette for those 'bleached flags!/ . . . – Rags or ragged garments/ hung on the chairs and hooks', she switches abruptly to 'cruel' black as soon as Faustina approaches.

It may be worth noting, too, that whenever this poet turned her mind to appeasing her social conscience – whenever she *knew* she was writing not only from personal experience but from observations relating to serious moral issues, she tended to choose tight forms and demanding stanza patterns. Crashaw provided a ready-made stanza for 'Roosters'. The seven-line, basically three-stress stanza she adopted for 'Faustina' was doubtless, too, a disciplinary device. Counting out three accents per line for six lines before ending each stanza with a two-stress coda distracted her from too obviously showing her feelings. A recently published volume of Bishop's paintings, *Exchanging Hats*, suggests that for Bishop, painting may have been a more desirable medium of expression, though she was too self-critical to take her (very attractive) amateur watercolours seriously as art.[9]

Elizabeth Bishop was furiously upset by what she saw of racial exploitation in America's Deep South, as she was later by the inhuman treatment of the poor by the privileged rich in Rio de Janeiro; yet she rarely permitted herself to give vent to her anger directly.* 'Jerónimo's House', 'Faustina' and Part IV of 'Songs for a Colored Singer' beautifully convey the poet's pity for and

---

* An exception to this rule is the bitterly cynical 'Pink Dog', not published in Bishop's lifetime.

empathy with the poor black population of Florida. The popular ballad, 'The Burgler of Babylon', with the more subtle lyric, 'Squatter's Children', carry that sympathetic empathy to Brazil. But in all these poems, strong discipline in the writing stiffens the sentiments displayed, as though the poet were afraid of giving offence through condescension. 'Squatter's Children' is typical of Bishop's skill in this respect. The poem is crucial on many counts, and it pays to read it several times. In it, Bishop's restless, thinking eye picks out on some 'unbreathing' hills, probably around Petrópolis, two 'specklike' immigrant children, with their little dog, playing with their father's broken mattock outside their 'specklike', evidently homemade house.

The scene is once more painterly, with a storm piling up as the children's laughter 'spreads/ effulgence in the thunderheads'. Laughter, however, cannot preserve them in the 'little, soluble, unwarrantable ark' of their make-believe, for their Mother's voice (the upper-case M is important) 'ugly as sin/ keeps calling to them to come in.' In the final stanza, the poet, noting the children's reluctance to obey their mother and come in out of the rain, addresses them wistfully:

> Children, the threshold of the storm
> has slid beneath your muddy shoes;
> wet and beguiled, you stand among
> the mansions you may choose
> out of a bigger house than yours,
> whose lawfulness endures.
> Its soggy documents retain
> your rights in rooms of falling rain.

On a literal level, 'Squatter's Children' is little more than a sketch, a glimpse of poverty that, after all, is not *too* bad, though it is hardly possible to miss the poem's resounding 'echolalia'. As in 'Little Exercise', a conceptual schism is perceived to divide natural happenings – the 'unbreathing' hills, a storm piling up –

from human beings, who can choose to be part of nature, or at war with it, or, like the innocent man asleep in his rowboat, indifferent or blind to the peril of the situation. In Bishop's view, the squatter's children, by ignoring Mother's command and choosing to stay out in the rain, have elected to live in nature's 'bigger house'. The reference in the line 'the mansions you may choose' must be biblical, 'In my Father's house are many mansions,' though Bishop was not a Christian believer, and one must take 'mansions' here to mean nature's, not God's. Nevertheless, her poem states emphatically that in nature's big outdoor house 'lawfulness endures.' The 'soggy documents' that retain the children's rights in 'rooms of falling rain' are cruel, natural laws. 'You may choose to stay out in the rain, children,' says the poet *sotto voce*, 'but if you do, you'll get wet!' In the language of Bishop's short story, 'The Country Mouse', these squatter's children are truly 'in for it!'. They remind her of herself as a child, who with the fearful figure of her mother out of sight, yet still 'calling' in the background, once asked herself grimly in a dentist's waiting room:

How had I got tricked [beguiled] into such a false position? I would be like that [Mother-like] woman opposite who smiled at me so falsely... 'You are you,' something said. 'How strange you are, inside looking out. You are not Beppo [the pup], or the chestnut tree, or Emma, you are you and you are going to be you forever.' It was like coasting down hill, this thought, only much worse, and it quickly smashed into a tree. Why was I a human being?

The same question, 'Why was I a human being?' is overheard smashing into further trees in 'Squatter's Children'. Why are these children human? What exactly is their evolutionary position? Given their innocence and grinding poverty, what sad choices does the future hold for them? Disturbing in context is the upper case 'M' in the line, 'Mother's voice, ugly as sin'. Although 'Mother' here may well reflect Bishop's suspicious attitude towards mothers in general (and especially her own) the capitalised noun was probably intended to introduce the idea of Mother Church – Brazil's repressive Roman Catholic religion. 'Mother', here, certainly cannot represent Mother Earth, against whom Mother Church, in Bishop's view, *sins* by preaching to a hopelessly poor and disadvantaged population a false doctrine of eternal happiness for 'good' obedient people in Heaven.

*   *   *

'Squatter's Children' is one of ten Brazilian poems Elizabeth Bishop completed between July 1955, when Houghton Mifflin in Boston published Poems: *North & South – A Cold Spring*, and November 1965, when the New York firm of Farrar, Straus and Giroux brought out her third collection, *Questions of Travel*.* Like the 1955 collection, the original edition of *Questions of Travel* divided naturally into three sections. The first consisted of eleven poems written and set in Brazil. The second, modelled on Robert Lowell's *Life Studies*, republished Bishop's autobiographical 'In the Village', the story pivotal to all her work. A final section, 'Elsewhere', consisted of three important poems relating to Bishop's childhood ('Manners', 'Sestina' and 'First Death in Nova Scotia') followed by five further poems connected by the thread of her travels and her process of self-recovery through memory.

For any other poet, nineteen poems and a short story would have seemed a poor show for fifteen years' labour; and indeed, as Lota de Macedo Soares too often reminded her, Elizabeth Bishop was unable to keep up the pace of more facile writers. The entire corpus of her work has to be understood as the record of one hypersensitive person's cautious, watchful, self-conscious inching towards the truth. It asks to be read as autobiography, but as

---

* Elizabeth Bishop's first Brazilian poem was 'Arriveal at Santos' written in 1952 and originally printed as the final poem in *A Cold Spring*. It made good sense to reprint it ten years later as the first poem in *Question of Travel*.

an autobiography told from the 'inside looking out.' Instead of a year-by-year chronicle of a life, we are given a series of impressions or 'looks' – a slide-show of places, people, creatures and small events, all of which have been seen, enacted and carefully noted down to be carried ever afterwards in the clear mirror of the writer's memory: 'As if a river should carry all/ the scenes that it had once reflected/ shut in its waters, and not floating/ on momentary surfaces.'*

A factor at least as inhibiting to Elizabeth Bishop as her relentless truth-seeking was her apparent inability to write very much without pursuing the line of ontological-cum-epistemological questioning she had laid bare 'in the waiting room' of childhood. This line we can see multiplying and extending itself in 'Squatter's Children', running back through 'Questions of Travel' and 'Arrival at Santos' to 'The Bight', 'At the Fishhouses' and 'Cape Breton', among other major poems. It must be confessed that any bestowing of abstract terminology on Elizabeth Bishop is, to say the least, risky. Bishop herself claimed that she had always been weak in philosophy, and she rarely, in any case, favoured 'grand, all-out efforts.'[11] In many ways, such a disclaimer was a form of self-protection masquerading as snobbery. Bishop didn't, in general, approve of academics who tried to explain or take over poetry, and she positively loathed aesthetic arguments, agreeing with Wordsworth that if you can't say something in everyday words, it is probably not worth saying. Conversely, categorically unanswerable questions such as *what is a human being?*, *what is knowledge?*, *what choices are we given in this life?*, *what is there in the world that makes it it, and people people?* must at some time, she thought, occur to everybody. Why muddy deep waters with useless discussion? Why not just look?

It is, of course, one thing to ask 'big' questions in plain language, another to answer them. No more than any other

* See 'The Weed', *Collected Poems*, pp. 20–21.

enquiring stoic could Bishop articulate her idea of being in the abstract. She could only speak truthfully about being somewhere, at a certain time. Nor do her poems, as a rule, provide more than signposts pointing to temporary resting places, and these, most of them, are actual places solidly perceived and situated. At their most convincing, Bishop's geographical poems begin in a low-keyed deictic mood, pointing at this and that. They go on so long, pointing and looking so intently that, by the end, some more abstract impression has to be felt. Only rarely, however, is this abstract idea identified, and even then it is often formulated as a question or a set of questions.

Lines that typically introduce Bishop's geographical excursions include these from 'At the Fishhouses': 'Although it is a cold evening,/ down by one of the fishhouses/ an old man sits netting,/ his net, in the gloaming almost invisible,/ a dark purple brown,/ and his shuttle worn and polished; and these from 'Cape Breton': 'Out on the high 'bird islands,' Ciboux and Hertford,/ the razorbill auks and the silly-looking puffins all stand/ with their backs to the mainland/ in solemn, uneven lines along the cliff's brown grass-frayed edge/ '; and these from 'Questions of Travel': 'There are too many waterfalls here; the crowded streams/ hurry too rapidly down to the sea,/ and the pressure of so many clouds on the mountaintops/ makes them spill over the sides in soft slowmotion,/ turning to waterfalls under our very eyes.' No writing could seem more natural than the loose weave of these passages, all of which would be prose if some bodiless pressure – like those clouds on the Brazilian mountaintops – were not making them spill over. For by the time they draw to an end, all three poems, through some act of verbal alchemy, have struck something rich and strange – as much by virtue of what is not said as by what is. 'At the Fishhouses' is exceptional in that 'knowledge' is actually named, though not until a trance-inducing incantation has prepared for it:

> The water seems suspended
> above the rounded gray and blue-gray stones.
> I have seen it over and over, the same sea, the same,
> slightly, indifferently swinging above the stones,
> icily free above the stones,
> above the stones and then the world.

A dreamy hypnotic effect is achieved by the repetition of 's' sounds: seems, suspended, stones, same, sea, same, slightly, swinging, stones, icily, stones, stones. As the passage progresses, the words slowly work themselves closer and closer to the elements: water, stones, sea, stones, the sea icily swinging 'above the stones and then [above] the world', anticipating the world's ultimate and inevitable destruction – 'as if the water were a transmutation of fire/ that feeds on stones and burns with a dark gray flame.' Earth, air, fire, water: these are the elements of knowledge, or rather more carefully, 'what we *imagine* knowledge to be' (my italics). For finally, 'At the Fishhouses' throws the world back at imagination. The speaker, looking for herself and losing herself in a geography, is returned to the ever-passing mirror of her own mind:

> It is like what we imagine knowledge to be:
> dark, salt, clear, moving, utterly free,
> drawn from the cold hard mouth
> of the world, derived from the rocky breasts
> forever, flowing and drawn, and since
> our knowledge is historical, flowing, and flown.

It is no wonder Eliabeth Bishop was impatient of philosophy with its much less precise, less 'real' vocabulary of argument and definition. All the same, only a very few of her poems achieve conclusions that do not either imply or directly raise abstract questions. Often, as at the end of 'Cape Breton', things simply continue in their cloud of unknowing: 'The bird keeps on singing;

a calf bawls, the bus starts./ The thin mist follows/ the white mutations of its dream . . . ' Mist, as also in 'Sandpiper', indicates that language can take us no further. 'Twelfth Morning: or What You Will' begins 'Like a first coat of whitewash when it's wet,/ the thin gray mist lets everything show through', allowing the mist to question the confidence of the 'black boy Balthazar' who boasts like the Wiseman he isn't, 'that the world's a pearl, and I, I am / its highlight!' Ignorant boy! chuckles the poet, not without sympathy.

'Questions of Travel' begins with a long look at geological time, introducing the tiny dimension of human time with a series of personal questions. 'Should we have stayed at home and thought of here?/ Where should we be today?/ Is it right to be watching strangers in a play/ in this strangest of theatres?/ What childishness [makes us] determined to rush/ to see the sun the other way around?' Turning these questions over, putting the other side ('But surely it would have been a pity/ not to have seen' these trees, this gas station, those bird-cages; not to have heard this rain 'like politician's speeches') leads to further questions; and these again touch on the significance of imagination and choice:

> Is it lack of imagination that makes us come
> to imagined places, not just stay at home?
> Or could Pascal have been not entirely right
> about just sitting quietly in one's room?
>
> Continent, city, country, society:
> the choice is never wide and never free.
> And here, or there . . . No. Should we have stayed at home,
> wherever that may be?

Here are set down the principal questions underlying the poems of Bishop's later years – and often earlier ones, too. First (and yet again), what is imagination and how best can it lead to the truth? Is it an act of intense concentration or fantastic escape or both? Does our search for what matters gain most from quietly thinking in a room or from rushing across the world 'to see the sun the other way around?' Secondly, both contemplation and action offer advantages, but in opting for action, did 'we' (she) have a choice? Was an imagined alternative life ever possible? Can we choose where to go and how to live, or are we set in predestined ways more or less from childhood? Finally, and most crucially for Elizabeth Bishop, where and what is 'home'? 'Continent, city, country, society'? What difference can it ultimately make to any of us (our lives are so brief) to belong to one place or to one set of people rather than another? The wistfulness of that last 'wherever that may be?' suggests that for Bishop 'home' was the sacrifice she had had to make in order to become the woman and artist she was. Because she had chosen to be independent, because it had been open to her not to compromise with convention and not to marry (as she might have had to do in less privileged circumstances or in former years), of her own volition she had blown up all her routes home. The world of her past in Nova Scotia and even in Massachusetts was gone for ever. Unless, of course, she could recreate it in imagination, in art.

Before Bishop went to live in Brazil, she had spent two stretches of time at Yaddo, the artists' colony in Saratoga Springs, New York. During her second visit there, in the winter of 1950, she completed a double sonnet (a strict and challenging form) called 'The Prodigal' – later collected in *A Cold Spring*. 'The Prodigal', yet another poem that draws from a biblical source, ends 'But it took him a long time/ finally to make his mind up to go home.' Though the poem's setting – in a filthy pigsty – is fictional, there is no doubt that Bishop's drunken Prodigal stood for herself; just as the pigsty represented her 'rotten' all but unsalvageable state of mind at the time. What is interesting in view of what came later, is that both the poem and the original parable give the Prodigal Son free will. He has a choice. He can stop drinking and go home if he wants to; and the implication of the parable is that he will be welcomed, that his sins will be forgiven.

It is important to see, then, how differently matters stand in 'Questions of Travel' – written when Bishop was happy and settled in a new home in Petrópolis, having already gone back 'home' to Nova Scotia (and forgiven herself?) in her two short stories and several poems. While writing 'The Prodigal' she could scarcely see over the horizon of her own misery. In reaching for her Bible, she was reaching for a faith (for her, now a fiction) that had served her grandparents, on both sides, and that grounded her, too, in Christian history. Before writing 'Questions of Travel', on the other hand, she had been absorbing herself in Charles Darwin's researches on The Beagle and Charles Wagley's studies of primitive tribes in Amazonia. She was in a position to take a long view of religion, history, ethnology and geology, and, above all, she no longer felt much personal guilt about what and where she was. Hence the joking tone in which she dismisses any egotistical claim to centrality:

> For if those streaks, those mile-long, shiny, tearstains,
> aren't waterfalls yet,
> in a quick age or so, as ages go here,
> they probably will be.

Metaphorically, wistfulness is still expressed, of course: 'tearstains' gives the poet away, matching waterfalls with tears. But the poem makes nothing of these tears and everything of the speaker's fascination with a new geography and a new world that does, in fact, give a positive answer to the ironical question raised in 'Arrival at Santos': 'Oh, tourist,/ is this how this country is going to answer you/ and your immodest demands for a different world,/ and a better life, and complete comprehension of both at last . . . ?'

It is, in fact, precisely the juxtaposition of personal, geological and historical perspectives in these Brazilian poems that, in setting up a drama of opposites, gives them life. Written as monologues, they point to situations that are in themselves dialectical. Furthermore, all these poems are addressed to somebody. Like George

Herbert, Bishop casts herself in the role of interlocutor, and her wonder at nature was not unlike Herbert's apprehension of God. Sometimes Bishop speaks intimately to her readers, treating them to a moment by moment account of natural marvels. Sometimes, as in 'Manuelzinho' and 'The Riverman', she assumes the voice of a specific persona: Lota de Macedo Soares in the first instance, an Amazonian Indian in the second. In 'Brazil, January 1, 1502' the poet assumes responsibility for her contemporaries' ignorance (note that telltale 'our' in the opening line) in the lushest of landscapes that appears still to be virgin but which in fact was deflowered more than four hundred years ago with the arrival of the conquistadors. Here, again, the Brazilian geography – gorgeous and self-sufficient – provides a setting for the natural 'Sin' the colonising European Catholics set out to destroy; and are still, in the name of commerce and religion, committing the ethnic and ecological sin of exploiting.

It was while she was visiting Nova Scotia in 1946 that Bishop first struck upon the phrase 'the geographical mirror'. She was making notes at the time for 'At the Fishhouses', describing 'the dark icy, clear water – clear dark glass' as 'my idea of knowledge, this cold stream, half drawn, half flowing from a great rocky breast.' In her biography of Bishop, Brett Millier inferred from these jottings that the poet had begun looking for herself in the mirror of the landscape (see note 5). And it is probably true to say that Bishop's geographical poems are essentially exercises in self-placement. Mirrors, however, throughout her work pretty consistently stand for the imagination. Her New York poems of the '30s and '40s conceive of a looking-glass world that corrects or reverses the real one. In 'The Gentleman of Shalott', 'From the Country to the City' and 'Insomnia', mirrors represent aspects of a divided consciousness; in 'Love Lies Sleeping' and 'The Man-Moth', they feature as alien eyes or tears; in 'The Weed', they retain memories in drops of river-water. But with 'At the Fishhouses' – and even earlier, in 'Florida' – a shift of emphasis grants geography the central position formerly occupied by glass. Immediately, the question arises: which is the mirror in these geographical imaginings, the poet or the geography? Did the poet looking for herself in the landscape of 'At the Fishhouses' expect to find an image of herself 'out there'? Or did she realize that the act of looking is always reflective? No matter how intently she searched nature for an identity, she could see only what her eye and mind perceived. Geography could provide her with no more than a reflection in the transparent glass of her own polished window.

As we have seen, those last, marvellous lines of 'At the Fishhouses' do acknowledge the limitations of the senses: 'It is like what we *imagine* knowledge to be'. The world, in other words, is vastly larger and more mysterious than anything we catch hold of in our mental mirrors. Though 'At the Fishhouses' takes place as far as possible 'out there', away from the poet's psyche, it is nevertheless a poem of self-recognition.

CHAPTER FIVE

Geography III

'Because of my era, sex, situation, education, etc., I have
written, so far, what I feel is a rather 'precious' kind of poetry,
although I am very much opposed to the precious. One wishes
things were different, that one could begin all over again.'
                    Elizabeth Bishop, letter of 8 January 1964

Mary McCarthy, contributing to a symposium in the *New York
Times Book Review*, once wrote of Elizabeth Bishop, 'I envy the
mind hiding in her words, like an 'I' counting up to a hundred
waiting to be found.'[1] Yet Bishop herself, with a characteristic show
of modesty, counted only up to three. The title of her fourth and
last slim volume claims for its author only third-grade status as a
student of geography, suggesting that in her opinion she had
struggled through the first and second grades fairly successfully. As
if to emphasise that she still felt herself to be at an elementary stage
of learning, Bishop introduced *Geography III* (1976) with a series
of quotations from a schoolbook of 1884: '*What is Geography? A
description of the earth's surface. What is the Earth? The planet or
body on which we live . . . What is a Map? A picture of the whole,
or a part, of the Earth's surface. In what direction from the center of
the picture is the Island? . . . In what direction is the Volcano? The
Cape? The Bay? The Lakes? The Strait?*'. It's as if, with this eruption
of naïve questions and answers, Bishop were telling us that
geography makes a better base for poetry than self-expression or
personal confession, and we ought to start by looking around at
where we are. This impression is not quite borne out by the

contents of her book. Although 'The Moose', 'Poem' and 'The End of March' are scrupulously placed, none of the nine new poems Bishop published in *Geography III* engages in the kind of stone-by-stone, leaf-by-leaf explorations undertaken in, say, 'Cape Breton' or 'Brazil, January 1, 1502'. The geographies in this final volume lie in the mind of the poet and for the most part (like the poems set 'Elsewhere' in *Questions of Travel*) are geographies of memory and imagination.

Between 1965 (*Questions of Travel*) and 1970, when she began to teach at Harvard, Elizabeth Bishop suffered and survived a series of personal upheavals that cut her off forever from her Brazilian Eden. At the end of 1960, Carlos Lacerda, the newly elected governor of Guanabara State, had appointed Lota de Macedo Soares to supervise the construction of a large people's park on the Rio waterfront. Elizabeth, with Lota, moved from Petrópolis to spend weekdays in Rio, fifty miles away. Despite the charm of their penthouse apartment overlooking the Copacabana Beach, Bishop began to suffer from feelings of neglect as Lota's time was more and more absorbed by management difficulties and Byzantine Brazilian politics. In 1965, despairing of reviving their life together in the country, Bishop accepted an invitation to teach from January to June, 1966, at the University of Washington in Seattle. On returning to Brazil late in June, she found Lota jealous, irritable and ill from overwork. A trip to Amsterdam and London in the fall had to be cut short when Lota broke down.

In May, 1967, Bishop set off alone by sternwheeler down the Rio São Francisco to gather information for a book she'd been commissioned to write on Brazil, and in June she was back in Petrópolis. By that time, Lacerda was no longer in power and Lota had been overruled and supplanted as supervisor of the almost-completed park. Her resultant state of acute nervous prostration induced Elizabeth to put distance between them. She flew to New York in July 1967, taking refuge in a friend's empty apartment in Greenwich Village. In September, against her doctor's advice, Lota followed Elizabeth to New York; in the early morning after the day of her arrival, she committed suicide. Bishop, who, in the previous year, had bought and was restoring an eighteenth-century house in the picturesque town of Ouro Prêto in Minas Gerais, was forced in the succeeding months to acknowledge that Brazil no longer could or would offer her a home.

Elizabeth Bishop's return to the United States coincided with the onset of the Vietnam War and its concomitant youth revolution at the end of the 1960s. For a year Bishop lived with a young woman and her child in San Francisco, where her writing trickled to a halt, though she continued to translate Brazilian poetry, co-editing an *Anthology of Twentieth-Century Brazilian Poetry* with Emanuel Brasil. In 1968 she received the National Book Award for her (first) *Complete Poems*, thereafter picking up an astounding number of literary prizes, climaxing in the Neustadt International Prize for Literature in 1976. On December 28 of that same year – when Elizabeth Bishop was settled in Boston and teaching at Harvard – Farrar, Straus and Giroux published *Geography III*. It was, she thought, a distressingly thin collection, containing only nine poems and a translation; and yet as usual, its quantitative meagreness was more than made up for by the excellence of its contents. Each one of these nine poems reaches back to reassess and rework ideas that had animated her earlier writing, while four or five extend the comparative narrowness of her range from the personal to what has to be termed the universal. The unforgettable poems of *Geography III* behave like searchlights, beginning at a tiny point in the writer's experience, then slowly widening out into great horns of illumination. Poem by poem, the book yields an overview of this poet's late plainspeaking, factually faithful, hard-earned grasp of as much truth as she could lay hold of.

Opening with 'In the Waiting Room' (discussed at length in Chapter One), Bishop once again confirmed her poetry's source in childhood. The dreadful yet fruitful effect of that 'vastation' in the dentist's waiting room had remained with her over the years:

'nothing stranger/ had ever happened nothing/ stranger could ever happen.' The autobiographical frankness of 'In the Waiting Room' prepares the way for the next poem, 'Crusoe in England', which extends and deepens the parable-like technique Bishop employed in 'The Prodigal'. Robinson Crusoe, happily, is a far wittier, more emotionally detached substitute for Bishop than her almost-self-justifying Prodigal Son. One might even say that Bishop's Crusoe is the Prodigal come home at last, settled, forgiven, and yet somehow disappointed, let down. Looking back at the unrepeatable experiences of his island exile, this prodigal Crusoe realises how truly strange they were, yet how unique and incommunicable to the well-meaning inhabitants of 'England'. England could well stand, here, for the American universities that in the 1970s were tumbling over one another in their eagerness to give Bishop honourary degrees. None of the collector-professors, of course, ever got the point. How could they? All Crusoe-Bishop can leave them for their academic museum are 'home-made' relics of a private, undiscoverable geography and a difficult art. Inventions once precious to herself because they had enabled her to survive would mean almost nothing to theorising academics:

> the flute, the knife, the shrivelled shoes,
> my shedding goatskin trousers
> (moths have got in the fur),
> the parasol that took me such a time
> remembering the way the ribs should go.
> It still will work but, folded up,
> looks like a plucked and skinny fowl,
> How can anyone want such things?

In 'Crusoe in England', Elizabeth Bishop plays over the motifs of her search for a viable self that began in the 1930s with 'The Sea & Its Shore' and 'In Prison'. By the 1970s, she had become even better at viewing her mental and physical adventures with incredulous, cool, fond amusement. Even Lota, represented by Friday in the poem, recedes into the dulled pain of the irrecoverable: 'And Friday, my dear Friday, died of measles/seventeen years ago come March.'

This impression of near-flippancy regarding Lota, for whom Elizabeth, in 1979, was planning to write a serious book-length elegy, is belied in 'Five Flights Up', the final (original) poem in *Geography III*, in which an almost insupportable past is rendered bearable by being set in something like the perpetual present. Writing yet again about waking up, or lying awake, the poet this time turns her back on her imagination, and instead of indulging her dreams, resolutely confronts them with time *now*, in an ordinary room on an ordinary morning. Life goes on, the world is, despite the terrible things human beings think up and do to one another. The unknown bird and the little dog in 'Five Flights Up' are minor versions of the moose; they call attention to the otherness in which we suffer – an otherness that ultimately absorbs suffering through indifference, opening a door in the dark through which we pass to go on living. Where we ultimately pass to is not something Bishop wished to speculate about; but in 'Five Flights Up' we observe her picking herself up once more and wearily setting off for 'the dark ajar'.

With 'The Moose' completed after twenty-five years' labour (see Chapter Three) and confirmed by the achievement of 'Five Flights Up', Bishop had said all she wished to say, or perhaps could say, about her ontological position. Acting according to an aesthetic rule she had laid down for herself in her late twenties, she had more than succeeded in 'The Moose' in drawing something 'spiritual' out of her 'material', and in so doing, had neither bowed to the doctrines of a religious faith nor abandoned her practical curiosity about the world. A modern transcendentalist? Yes, perhaps. Yet by faithfully adhering *first* to her material she had single-handedly renewed, hardened and refreshed – with her common-sense wit – that profoundly entrenched American tradition. In *Geography III*, for instance, 'The End of March' covertly acknowledges a co-inheritor in Wallace Stevens by calling him to account for his overfondness for imaginary abstractions. Where Stevens wrote of the sun with romantic panache as the 'lion of the spirit' that in poetry is a 'destructive force', Bishop chose to recast the animal as domestic and dog-like, a player with imaginary kites. Some critics have suggested that this poem makes a sly reference to Stevens's 'Sea Surface Full of Clouds'. Having looked very carefully at that cold March sea in Massachusetts, Bishop observed that 'The sky was darker than the water/ – it was the color of mutton-fat jade.' The italicised it, draws attention to the Stevens-like image, but as Bishop maintains in a letter to Jerome Mazzaro 'the water was the color of mutton-fat jade.' She was merely telling the truth.

Playful as the tone of 'The End of March' appears to be, the poem is the last in a series scattered throughout Bishop's work on the theme of desirable houses. From Edwin Boomer's shack in 'The Sea & Its Shore' through 'The Monument' guarding the bones of its artist-prince, to 'Jerónimo's House', to the child's drawing in 'Sestina', to the specklike hovel in 'Squatter's Children', houses in Elizabeth Bishop's poems represent frail refuges for the imagination, perilous retreats from the world's hurricanes in which to 'think'. The proto-crypto-dream-house on the beach in 'The End of March' is no exception. More than any of these other houses it resembles the author's cell in 'In Prison' – a place where a writer might ideally retire and, uncriticised, do nothing, 'look through binoculars, read boring books . . . and write down useless notes.' The point is not that such a house is all one ought to need (Elizabeth Bishop was certainly no hippy or new-age traveller); it's more the untroubled spiritual home most writers aspire to but never find. For Bishop, who rarely felt at ease in the world and for whom living was sometimes torture, a life of freedom to be ordinary was a crypto-dream she only rarely realised. Nor could she reach her dream-house on that freezing March day in Duxbury. Even if she had, the dream would have been boarded up and inaccessible. At the end of the poem, she and her dedicatees, John

Malcolm Brinnin and Bill Read (writers and homosexuals like
herself), are perforce refused the comforts even of this derelict
refuge and left, as ever, to the mercies of Stevens's destructive (but
Bishop's playful) lion sun and those drab, damp, momentarily
glorious, multi-coloured stones.[2]

Other fables, too, in *Geography III* round off and say goodbye to
past preoccupations. 'Night City' is an exercise in metaphysical
tropes as it bids farewell to New York and, by extension, to every
modern city's dehumanising spectacle of violence, waste, guilt,
'light-pollution' (she didn't yet have the term) and vast, commer-
cial greed. Looking down from a plane, she watches a city 'burn
tears, burn guilt':

> A pool of bitumen
> one tycoon
> wept by himself,
> a blackened moon.
>
> Another cried
> a skyscraper up.
> Look! Incandescent,
> its wires drip.

In a familiar Bishopian image conflating tears (or rain), birds and
falling wires, 'Night City' plays a final variation on a nightmare
theme of the 1930s (see 'Some Dreams They Forgot' of 1933).
Bishop brought the same image into the obscure dreaminess of
'Rain Towards Morning' towards the end of *A Cold Spring*. 'Night
City' substitutes a flock of 'careful' planes for the frightening birds
of her nightmare, ending ironically with a doubtful gleam of hope.
Note the parenthesis:

> (Still there are creatures.
> careful ones, overhead.
> They set down their feet, they walk
> green, red; green, red.)

The whimsical, mock-journalese of '12 O'clock News' reaches even further back into Bishop's past, drawing on notes Bishop made at Vassar for a *jeu d'esprit* on the eerie, isolated, even-then-defensive geography of writers and writing. Speaking as a broadcaster on assignment in a strange, embattled country, she describes a secret landscape not unlike the exile's island colonised by Crusoe. The writer's moon-like lamp, typewriter, pile of manu-scripts, sheets of paper, envelopes, ink-bottle, typewriter eraser and ashtray all invite suspicion, taking on the significance of a subversive country's defences under siege. Here is a language-land struggling to survive in and even capture a huge universe of armed happenings. Its heroism, of course, is hopeless. The heaped pile of dead soldier-cigarettes lying in the crater-ashtray, inappropriately clad in white for warfare in the mind's mountains, give conclusive evidence either of 'the childishness and hopeless impracticality of this inscrutable people, *our opponents*, or of the sad corruption of their leaders.' (My italics.)

The tongue-in-cheek satire makes fun of the pretensions of leading writers while mocking the gullibility of the reporters who insensitively pursue them. In context, 'our opponents' gives the game away, betraying the poet's ironic contempt for the speaker and indirectly drawing attention to the same unbridgeable gulf dividing artists from philistines that gave substance to 'A Word with You' back in 1933. That Bishop chose to rework and complete '12 O'clock News' for *Geography III* suggests that her aesthetic snobbishness (her word) had not abated over the years. It is likely that she held in contempt a good many of the well-meaning prize-givers and interviewers (how could they possibly understand what she'd been through?) who, in her last years, were responsible for her fame.

Reversing, in many ways, the joking élitism of '12 O'clock News', the more famous 'One Art' – Bishop's single, wholly triumphant villanelle – directly addresses the theme of loss that runs obscurely, like a chill current, through all her work, even at its wittiest. Towards the end of her life, Bishop apparently still considered the pain of her personal deprivations to be unassuaged, yet she had written what she had written, and her work, she knew, would survive. A justified pride, then, compels the iteration of losses in 'One Art': first her mother's watch (note the double meaning of 'watch'), then Nova Scotia, then Key West and her beautiful house there, then Lota and two 'loved' houses in Brazil, then Brazil itself with its superb rivers, and finally the anticipated (but never, fortunately, actual) loss of Alice Methfessel, the friend with whom Elizabeth shared the last decade of her life. Though each loss was dreadful at the time, the poem declares, none were actually disasters if losing is an 'art' indispensable to the art of *writing*: 'the art of losing's not too hard to master/ though it may look like (*Write* it!) like disaster.' 'Write it' asks, too, to be read as '*right* it'; to write something is to right it. Thus a poem begun in despair became, through successive and painful revisions, a poem about the triumph of poetry – *Mount Despair* becoming, in the crucible of Bishop's one art, *Mont d'Espoir*.

Such a proposal concerning the saving properties of art makes no provision, of course, for non-artists. What are less gifted people to do about their losses? The implication is that the untalented will find solace in the art of others – though in truth, Elizabeth Bishop never gave much thought to the plight of second-raters. Although she felt infinite compassion for the poor and always retained her affinity with children and animals, she was openly contemptuous of people she considered dull, vain, intellectually pretentious or, worst of all, unobservant. Her sometimes unjustified prejudices were curbed – most of the time – by a natural generosity that collapsed only when she felt disregarded or personally criticised. Indeed, a subtitle for her *Complete Poems* could well be 'Strategies for Survival', and the occasional unkindness or rank élitism that surfaces in her work (that inability to like *anything* written or said about her for very long) must be understood as a tactic she perfected to keep her art alive and fighting.

Another stratagem, as we have seen, grounded itself in her idea of the geographical mirror – the mirror that nature holds up to us all in the form of on-going life continuing indifferently outside the bastions of our self-importance. This strategy, conspicuous in the art governing 'At the Fishhouses', 'Cape Breton', 'The Bight' and 'The Moose', perhaps finds its most personal expression in a poem significantly called 'Poem' which, in effect, fixes the parameters of all Bishop's late, thoughtful poems: 'life and the memory of it' mirroring each other in every form of art she thought worth preserving.

Art, of course, or rather *questions* of art, underlay many of Bishop's early, quasi-surrealistic achievements: 'The Map', 'The Imaginary Iceberg', 'Large Bad Picture' and 'The Monument'. But in these poems, fine as they are, dreams or life-avoiding ideas took the place of the geographies that so wonderfully sustain her later work. Now in 'Poem', written forty years after 'The Imaginary Iceberg', the question of what art is or should be has found, if not an answer, at least a sure approach to the question. (*Geography III*, after all!) It is an approach that gathers in and simplifies Bishop's ubiquitous questions of travel, as also (though she might have denied this) her stated and unstated ontological quest: the questions of being she found herself asking as a child in the dentist's waiting room. How Bishop, without setting out to achieve a masterpiece in 'Poem', was able to draw all these, questing lines together, I just don't know. The magic mirror that made such an act of art possible was a tiny oil painting by her great uncle, George Hutchinson, the painter also responsible for the 'Large Bad Picture'. Characteristically, 'Large Bad Picture' ends with an implied question, opening a door between the painting and a 'real-life' interpretation, but venturing no further into speculation:

Apparently [the painted ships] have reached their destination.
It would be hard to say what brought them there,
commerce or contemplation.

'Poem', as it were, begins where 'Large Bad Picture' ends, rejecting commerce ('this little painting . . . has never earned any money in its life') while openly engaging in contemplation. The informal, colloquial voice of the poet rambles from recognition of the place ('It must be Nova Scotia . . . ') to a description of the picture, to a recollected conversation with an aunt (all perfectly real) to a gentle, musing meditation on just about everything that matters. The gist of what she says is not original ('Ars Longa Vita Brevis') but as an expression of a felt connection between past and present, art and life, one time and all time, 'Poem' achieves something altogether surprising. Effortlessly, it makes a transition from the personal to the universal and from art to life, so that the reader feels intimately and immediately at home with the picture, the poem, the painter, the poet. For a moment, we are all 'just one'.

All these transformations and revelations happen naturally, without sounding in the least literary. It is as if the poet herself were 'talking the way they talked/ in the old featherbed,/ peacefully, on and on'. Her listeners are alike her lost great uncle, her present admirers and a host of future readers yet unborn:

> Our visions coincided – 'visions' is
> too serious a word – our looks, two looks:
> art 'copying from life' and life itself,
> life and the memory of it so compressed
> they've turned into each other. Which is which?

The question forks, still leaving us with a conundrum, but this time we are not allowed to escape the implications of what Elizabeth Bishop *really* wants us to hear: ' – the little that we get for free,/ the little of our earthly trust. Not much./ About the size of our abidance'. Isn't 'abidance' the perfect hymnlike word on which to end this little study of Elizabeth Bishop, whose 'look' continues to give hope, in art as in life, to 'the munching cows,/ the iris, crisp and shivering, the water/ still standing from spring freshets/ the yet-to-be-dismantled elms, the geese'?

Elizabeth Bishop: A Chronology

'When you write my epitaph, you must say I was the loneliest person who ever lived.'

Elizabeth Bishop to Robert Lowell in 1948, as reported by Robert Lowell, 15 August 1957

'I have a vague theory that one learns most – I have learned most – from having someone suddenly make fun of something one has taken seriously up until then. I mean about life, the world, and so on. This is again a form of snobbery.'

Elizabeth Bishop to Anne Stevenson, 8 January 1964

1911–14

Elizabeth Bishop [EB] was born on 8 February 1911, in Worcester, Massachusetts. Her father was William Thomas Bishop, eldest child of a contractor whose firm was responsible for a large number of public buildings in Boston and in the North-East of the United States. This John William Bishop, EB's paternal grandfather, had emigrated as a boy from Prince Edward Island, Canada, to work first in a cotton mill and later as a builder's assistant. An archetypal self-made man, he was successful enough by 1870 to marry in New York a Miss Sarah Foster from an old Massachusetts family. The Fosters traced their ancestry back to the New England settlers; in marrying into their family the *nouveau riche* J. W. Bishop was raising himself into what at that time passed in America for an aristocracy. However, in 1908, when Sarah and John's son William came to marry, he reconnected the prospering Bishops with the Maritime Provinces, choosing a comparatively poor Nova Scotian girl, Gertrude May Bulmer (locally pronounced Boomer), who had come to Boston to train as a nurse. William Bishop, a vice-president of his father's company and manager of the Worcester office, may have met his wife in hospital where he was being treated for Bright's disease. He died at thirty-nine, only three and a half years after his marriage, when EB was eight months old. Distraught by her husband's death, Gertrude Bulmer Bishop moved from Worcester into Boston to live with her sisters.

1915
After a period of hospitalisation for mental illness, Gertrude Bulmer Bishop returned with EB to her home in Great Village at the head of the Bay of Fundy in Nova Scotia. Her parents were William Brown Bulmer, formerly the village tanner, and his wife, Elizabeth Hutchinson (Bulmer) descended from an English family renowned for its sea captains and Baptist missionaries. A part of EB never ceased to identify with these maternal grandparents.

1916
In June, Gertrude Bulmer Bishop suffered a severe and (in those days) incurable mental breakdown. After a number of alarming incidents, Gertrude agreed to leave five-year-old EB with her family and enter a state sanatorium in Dartmouth, near Halifax. Her daughter never saw her again.

1917–22
After attending 'primer class' at the Great Village school, EB was, as she later put it, 'kidnapped' by her Bishop grandparents and brought back to join her unmarried aunt and uncle in the family's suburban farmhouse in Worcester. The child's unhappiness took the form of asthma, severe eczema and even, it seems, St Vitus Dance. Finally, in the spring of 1918, her grandfather took her to live with her mother's married sister, Aunt Maud Shepherdson, in

Revere, a run-down suburb of Boston. The Sheperdsons received money from the Bishops to help with expenses, and EB's health began to improve. She read all the poetry she could find on her aunt's shelves, attending local schools when her illnesses permitted. Until 1923, when her Bishop grandparents both died, she spent summers in Nova Scotia.

1923
EB's Uncle Jack (John Warren Bishop, 1880–1934) assumed responsibility for the annuity she had inherited from her father. The future poet tolerated but never liked either her Uncle Jack or his wife, Ruby. Nor did she have much time for her father's sister, Aunt Florence, the original of Aunt Consuelo in the poem 'In the Waiting Room'. Although the Bishops did what they considered 'right' by their niece, EB believed they were incapable of understanding her.

1924–27
At thirteen, EB went to a summer sailing camp, Camp Chequesset, in Wellfleet, Massachusetts. There she learned to sail and swim and made friends with girls of her own age. Discovering she could do things in the 'real' world, she enjoyed herself so much that she returned for five further summers, the last in 1929.

1927–30
Forced by ill health to repeat a year at a private school in Swampscott, EB was sixteen (a year older than most of her classmates) when she entered Walnut Hill, an academically demanding girls' boarding school in Natick, Massachusetts. After an unsettled year in the 10th grade, she began publishing poems and essays in the school magazine, *The Blue Pencil*. Eventually she made close (lifelong) friendships within a group of gifted, intelligent girls like herself.

1930–34

Graduating from Walnut Hill School in 1930, EB elected to follow her friend Frani Blough to Vassar (Woman's) College in Poughkeepsie, New York. There her close associates included Frani, who was studying music, Margaret Miller, a painter and art historian, and Louise Crane, who shared EB's passion for sailing, The future writer, Mary McCarthy, was a year ahead of her. In the summer of 1932, EB, with another friend went on a walking tour of Newfoundland. Back at Vassar in the autumn, EB and her 'modernist' contemporaries launched a radical literary magazine, *Con Spirito*, in which she published some heterodox but promising stories and poems. In her final (fourth) year at Vassar, EB co-edited the College Yearbook with Margaret Miller. Her famous meeting with the poet, Marianne Moore, took place on the right-hand bench outside the reading room of the New York Public Library on 16 March 1934. EB's mother died in her Dartmouth sanatorium the following May.

1934–36

EB graduated from Vassar in June of 1934. After a summer of sailing off the Massachusetts coast, she moved into a small apartment on the fringe of Greenwich Village in New York City. Sometime that winter, while suffering from flu and asthma, she wrote 'The Map'. In October 1935, 'The Map' appeared with 'Three Valentines' and 'The Reprimand' in an anthology called *Trial Balances*. Marianne Moore provided her young protégée with an eccentric but generous introduction.

In June of 1935, well before the publication of *Trial Balances*, EB set off with a Vassar friend on a German freighter bound for Belgium and France. After a stay in Douarnenez, where she translated poems by Rimbaud and Baudelaire, EB spent the winter in Paris with Louise Crane. Later, with Louise, she travelled to England, Morocco and Spain before returning to New York early in June of 1936. These were the travels she later recounted in 'Over 2000 Illustrations and a Complete Concordance'.

In November 1936, Elizabeth received news that Robert Seaver, a young man crippled with polio who for some years had wanted to marry her, had committed suicide.

1936–7
From December to January, EB and Louise Crane spent several weeks at a fishing resort in Naples, Florida. EB visited Key West for the first time over Christmas.

In June 1937, EB and Louise Crane set off for a second 'grand tour' of Europe, starting in Ireland. After meeting Margaret Miller in London, the three set off for Paris and the baroque churches of Burgundy. In mid-July, driving from Burgundy back to Paris, the girls' car, driven by Louise Crane, was forced off the road and overturned. EB and Louise got up uninjured, but Margaret Miller's right arm had been severed between elbow and wrist. After emergency proceedings had landed Margaret in the American Hospital in Paris, EB was left feeling guilty and helpless. She and Louise lingered in a Paris hotel until Margaret, in the care of her mother, was released from hospital. Then they travelled on, first to Arles and later (after EB had spent a week in the American Hospital with asthma) to Rome. Anxieties escalated before Louise Crane was tried for reckless driving in a French court late in October. Pronounced 'guilty', Crane paid a fine and was freed. After a short sightseeing tour of Italy (already arming itself for war) EB and Louise embarked for Boston from Genoa early in December and were back in the United States for Christmas.

1938–41
After spending the Christmas of 1937 with her Uncle and Aunt Shepherdson in Boston, EB moved back to New York. On her travels she had drafted 'The Monument' and two psychological fantasies, 'Sleeping on the Ceiling' and 'Sleeping Standing Up'. Yet when *The Partisan Review* asked her for work to accompany 'Love Lies Sleeping' in their January issue, she had nothing she thought was ready. She did, however, finish 'In Prison', which she sent to

a *Partisan Review* fiction competition in January. The story won a
$100 prize the following March.

In January 1938 EB moved, with her Uncle and Aunt
Shepherdson, to Key West, living for several months in a boarding
house run by a Mrs Pindar and later by a Miss Lula (whose coloured
maid was called Cootchie). In May, EB and Louise Crane bought
themselves a house at 624 White Street close to the town's Cuban
district. Gregorio Valdes, 'our new Key-West Rousseau', painted a
portrait of this house (see 'Gregorio Valdes' in the *Collected Prose*),
the first of the 'three loved houses' mentioned in 'One Art'. Among
the friends and artists EB met in Key West were the philosopher
John Dewey, and his daughter, Jane; the painter Loren MacIver,
and her poet husband Lloyd Frankenburg, and Ernest
Hemmingway's second wife, Pauline Pfeiffer Hemingway.

After moving into 624 White Street, EB flew to New York for the
summer, establishing the pattern of summering in the north and
wintering in Florida that gave her the title of her first book, *North
& South*. In 1938 she spent part of July and August in a shack on
a beach in Provincetown, Massachusetts. *The Partisan Review*
published 'Quai d'Orleans', 'The Unbeliever' and her first Key
West poem, 'Late Air' in July, and then 'Florida' in January. 'The
Monument' appeared in *New Directions Anthology* for 1939. A year
later (January 1940) 'Cirque d'Hiver', written in her beach shack
and originally titled 'Spleen', became the first of many EB poems
to appear in *The New Yorker*. Other Key West poems finished
between 1938 and 1940 can be directly related to her letters of the
time: 'Jerónimo's House', 'Seascape', 'Cootchie', 'The Fish' and
'Roosters'.

1938–40

In December 1938, EB joined Louise Crane for a week of canoeing
through Florida's Ten Thousand Islands, but EB never completed
the article she planned to write on the trip. She did, however, finish
'The Fish' that winter. In March 1940 it was published in *The*

Partisan Review, attracting the attention of Stanley Young at Harcourt Brace. Young invited her to submit a manuscript, but when she did, he advised her to wait until she had more poems. Although EB had effectively completed the manuscript she would later publish with Houghton Mifflin, she kept hoping to lengthen it into a longer, more 'serious' book. For the next five years EB's writing was more or less stymied: Harcourt Brace waited for new poems, while EB, disturbed and drinking too much, waited to hear more news from Harcourt Brace.

In October 1940, EB sent a draft of 'Roosters' to Marianne Moare and was surprised when Moore and her mother rewrote the poem. 'Roosters', in a version that Bishop revised only slightly, was published in a supplement to Edmund Wilson's *The New Republic* in April 1941. *Partisan Review* published what EB called her Key West 'tript-itch' ('Jerónimo's House', 'Cootchie' and 'Seascape') the following September.

1941–44
In the year EB turned thirty, World War II brought the U.S. Navy to Key West, and the cheerful insouciance of its population (so attractive to artists) came to an end. When Louise Crane left permanently to live in New York, EB rented her house to Navy personnel. In June 1941, she took up residence with a new companion, Marjorie Stevens, who worked as an accountant for the Navy.

From September to October of 1941, EB and Marjorie Stevens rented a cabin in the hill country of North Carolina. Then again in April 1942 they escaped the war mania to spend eight months exploring Mexico. There, climbing a pyramid near Merida, EB by accident met the Chilean poet, Pablo Neruda – of whose Communist poems she told Marianne Moore, she could not approve. Later Neruda's lyric 'Alberto Rojas Jimenez Viene Volando' became the model for EB's 'Invitation to Miss Marianne Moore' (published in 1948). The poem 'Anaphora' was begun on this trip but not finished until 1946 in Key West. After Marjorie Stevens died in 1959, Elizabeth dedicated 'Anaphora' to her.

In October 1942, EB returned alone to New York. Sometime that autumn, at Loren MacIver's studio on Perry Street in Greenwich Village, she was introduced to a Brazilian aristocrat and patronness of the arts called Maria Carlota de Macedo Soares. Companioned by Mary Stearns Morse, whom EB had met briefly in her college days, Lota de Macedo Soares – as she was always called – invited EB to visit them in Brazil should her travels take her to South America.

Back in Key West before Christmas 1942, EB remained there until the summer of 1944, writing little. For a week in August 1943, she took a job with the U.S. Navy, working in the optical shop grinding lenses, but had to give it up when the acids brought on eczema. She appears to have began writing again in November, drafting 'Large Bad Picture' and 'Songs for a Colored Singer'. In December, despite debilitating asthma, she began making notes for 'Faustina, or Rock Roses'.

In July 1944, asthma drove EB to New York again. She rented a tiny flat Loren MacIver had found for her on King Street – the setting for the dream-poem 'Varick Street' – and remained there until February 1945, though mostly she was too despairing to write. Her relationship with Marjorie Stevens tortured her, and she suffered continually from asthma. Trying to stop herself drinking, she went to a psychiatrist only to abandon her sessions after a few weeks. (In 1946, EB did receive some helpful psychiatric treatment from Dr Ruth Foster who, to EB's sorrow, died in 1950.) In September 1944, 'Songs for a Colored Singer' appeared in *The Partisan Review*; then in December, EB was jarred out of alcoholic misery by an invitation from an editor at Houghton Mifflin in Boston to submit a manuscript for its first annual Poetry Prize Fellowship. With Marianne Moore, John Dewey and Edmund Wilson for sponsors, she posted a typescript of *North & South* to Houghton Mifflin on 15 January 1945. A month later, she once more left New York City for Key West.

1945–46

Late in May 1945, EB received word that *North & South* had won her the Houghton Mifflin Literary Fellowship. The book remained unpublished, however, until August 1946, while she added final drafts of 'Anaphora' (published in *The Partisan Review* that autumn) 'Wading at Wellfleet', 'Chemin de Fer', 'Little Exercise' and 'Large Bad Picture' to her manuscript. The latter three poems appeared in *The New Yorker* in the spring of 1946. After delays and arguments with her publishers (EB hovered over the production, suggesting typefaces and last-minute revisions and corrections) an advance copy of the book reached her in Nova Scotia, where she was making notes for a poem that later became 'At the Fishhouses'. In a lonely, nerve-peeled state, she was deciding to stay on in Great Village when Marjorie Stevens summoned her back to the U.S. to sign the deed for her house sale in Key West. It seemed most convenient for EB to travel back to Boston by bus. This was the bus trip that twenty-six years later she immortalized in 'The Moose'.

1947

After one or two tepid reviews, *North & South* drew high praise from Marianne Moore in *The Nation*, Selden Rodman in *The New York Times Book Review* and Randall Jarrell in *The Partisan Review*. In January 1947, Jarrell introduced EB to Robert Lowell, whose review the following summer in *The Sewanee Review* pleased her by discerning 'two opposing factors' pulling against each other beneath the witty, observant surfaces of her poetry. Lowell's review reached EB when she was once again visiting Nova Scotia, this time staying with Marjorie Stevens in a farm-cum-guesthouse on Cape Breton. She and Lowell were soon exchanging letters and sending each other drafts of poems. As is well known, their close, not always easy friendship lasted until Lowell's death in 1977. EB must have begun writing 'Cape Breton' and 'A Summer's Dream' that summer – about the time 'At the Fishhouses' was published in *The New Yorker* on August 9.

On the strength of having won the Houghton Mifflin $1000 Poetry Prize, EB had received a Guggenhiem grant of $2,500 the previous April. She used the money partly to pay for her summer in Cape Breton. Returning to New York late in September, she made arrangements to interrupt her trip south with a visit to Washington DC where Robert Lowell was Poetry Consultant to the Library of Congress. In October, Lowell made recordings of EB reading her poems and introduced her to his then 'fiancée', a widow named Carley Dawson.

1947–48

As usual, EB spent the winter in Key West, working on 'Cape Breton', 'The Bight', 'Faustina, or Rock Roses' and 'Over 2000 Illustrations and a Complete Concordance'. On her way back to New York in May, she again stopped off in Washington to see Lowell. This time she went with him to visit Ezra Pound in St Elizabeth's Hospital. In June, EB set off for Wiscasset, Maine – by train, carrying a canary in a cage – but for some reason, probably to do with her drinking, Wiscasset 'proved to be a great mistake.' So in late July she removed with her visitor, Lowell's friend Carley Dawson, to Stonington where Lowell joined them. To EB's astonishment, Lowell dismissed Mrs Dawson, and after the poor woman left, the two poets spent an intimate day together, walking, swimming and later flying kites with another poet, Richard Eberhardt. In November, EB encountered Lowell again (as well as his second wife to be, Elizabeth Hardwick) at a poetry conference at Bard College. Years later, in 1957, after Lowell had married Elizabeth Hardwick and EB, with Lota de Macedo de Soares, had made a second visit to Stonington, Lowell wrote to tell EB that he'd assumed in 1948 that it 'would be just a matter of time before I proposed, and I half believed that you would accept.' Instead of asking EB to marry him, Lowell arranged for her to succeed Léonie Adams as Poetry Consultant to the Library of Congress for the year 1949–50.

1949

In February, having returned to Key West but no longer to Marjorie Stevens, EB and Virginia Pfeiffer (Pauline Hemingway's sister) set off for Haiti to be shown around the island by the critic and anthologist, Selden Rodman. After days of snorkling, sailing, spearfishing and generally finding her healthy self, EB felt better; but once back and living alone in Key West, despite progress with 'Cape Breton' and 'The Prodigal', she began to drink again. From May to July, she agreed to be treated for alcoholism at Blythdale in Greenwich, Connecticut. The rest of the summer she spent being lonely at Yaddo Artists' Colony in Saratoga Springs. News that Robert Lowell was about to marry Elizabeth Hardwick hit her especially hard. Between resumed drinking bouts, she sketched out a sequence of four poems which includes the hermetic 'While Someone Telephones'. According to Brett Millier, its first line was originally 'Your eyes, two darkened theatres/ in which I thought I saw you – saw you!/ but only played most miserably my doubled self.' EB was in no mental condition to live alone in Washington, DC.

Nevertheless, she took up her job as Consultant in Poetry at the Library of Congress in September. Predictably, she was unhappy in the post. Oppressed by Washington, reluctant to treat poetry as a 'business' and fearful of losing her friends, and even her New York doctor, through drink or bad behaviour, she disliked everywhere she tried to live. She found relief visiting Jane Dewey, who, though she worked as physicist testing ballistics for the Army, owned a cattle farm in Havre de Grace, Maryland. EB's letters of the autumn and winter of 1949 show her struggling with alcoholism and writing little. Reluctantly, she continued Lowell's practice of visiting Ezra Pound from time to time at St Elizabeth's. (See 'Visits to St Elizabeth's', CP p.133.) In the spring, between bouts of asthma, she recorded a reading by Dylan Thomas and began to make notes for the poem 'A Cold Spring', eventually dedicated to Jane Dewey. One day in late June she scribbled in her notebook 'The band playing on the steps of the Capitol – 1st sounds unreal, a sort of *imagined* band, then in short bursts, real,' and began to draft 'View of the Capitol from the Library of Congress'.

1950

EB's job at the Library of Congress continued through September, when, with relief, she handed the job over to Conrad Aiken. By October 1 she was back at Yaddo, struggling, as usual, with loneliness, asthma and alcoholism, but writing continuously. Her letters of November describe her living through a 'brainstorm', working on a 'perfectly endless story (never heard of again) having already sold eight new poems. Apart from 'A Cold Spring', Bishop's main achievement that winter was 'The Prodigal', which treats, in an oblique manner, of her own struggles with alcohol and her deferred return to Nova Scotia in 1946. ('The Prodigal' was published in *The New Yorker* on 17 March 1951.) Another achievement was 'O Breath'. At Yaddo that winter EB met Alfred Kazin and May Swenson and grew especially fond of the English painter Kit Barker and his German wife, Ilse (the novelist Kathrine Talbot). EB's homespun, witty correspondence with Kit and Ilse Barker continued until the end of her life.

1951-52

The first Lucy Martin Donnelly Fellowship from Bryn Mawr College was awarded to EB in March 1951, enabling her to get away from New York where, continually depressed, she still could not stop drinking. April found her once again visiting Jane Dewey in Maryland and completing 'A Cold Spring'. But in May, after receiving an American Academy of Arts and Letters Award in Washington, she returned to New York and slumped again. In the summer of 1951, EB returned to Nova Scotia where the Ottawa Lighthouse Authority had arranged for her to visit Sable Island, 'the graveyard of the Atlantic', where her great-grandfather Hutchinson's schooner had gone down with all hands. She spent two weeks of August on the island among the wild ponies and Ipswich Sparrows, walking over the dunes and making notes for a piece she intended to write for *The New Yorker*. Although her article got off to a promising start, she abandoned it after a few pages.

Back in New York in the autumn, Elizabeth considered joining the Lowells in Italy, only to be frustrated when the shipping company through which she had booked a round-the-world passage cancelled her ticket. Desperate to leave New York, she decided instead to take a cabin on a merchant ship bound for Tierra del Fuego and the Straits of Magellan; she would make her way up the West coast of South America and, following the *Beagle*'s route, get to Europe from the other side of world. On November 10, she boarded the S.S. *Bowplate*, which after eighteen days dropped her at the Brazilian port of Santos. EB spent two days in Sao Paulo before travelling by train to Rio de Janeiro where Mary Stearns Morse and Lota de Macedo Soares met her and made her welcome. After a sight-seeing tour of Rio, they drove her inland to see the modern house Lota was building on her family's estate near Petrópolis. Sometime around Christmas, EB suffered a violent allergic reaction from eating cashew fruit. When she recovered, she decided to remain in Brazil and share her life with Lota.

1952

In April, EB and Lota flew to New York to collect EB's books and belongings, say goodbye to an anxious Marianne Moore and fulfil EB's obligations under the Lucy Martin Donnelly Fellowship at Bryn Mawr College. EB received a Shelley Memorial Award of $800 in the autumn.

1953

'In the Village' and 'Gwendolyn' appeared *The New Yorker* (27 June and 19 December).

1954

EB was inducted into the (U.S.) National Institute of Arts and Letters. By this time, she was well into her translation from the

Portuguese of the Brazilian classic, *Minha Vida de Menina* (My Life as a Young Girl).

1955

On July 14, Houghton Mifflin published *Poems: North & South – A Cold Spring*, a reissue of EB's first book with the addition of twenty-one new poems.

1956

Poems: North & South – A Cold Spring was awarded the $500 Pulitzer Prize for Poetry. More lucrative was the $2700 *Partisan Review* Fellowship she won in the same year. Very happy in Lota's (and now her) ultra-modern house on the Samambaia Estate near Petrópolis, EB began translating Henrique Mindlin's *Modern Architecture in Brazil*.

1957

EB and Lota de Macedo Soares spent six months – April to October – in New York, subletting a small apartment on East 67th Street. They paid homage to Marianne Moore who turned seventy that summer, saw an uncountable number of friends and went to exhibitions – among them one of new paintings by Loren MacIver. The ostensible purpose of EB's visit was to discuss the production and correct proofs of *The Diary of Helena Morley* (the English title of *Minha Vida de Menina*; EB had wanted to call the diary *Black Beans and Diamonds*), published by Farrar, Straus and Cudahy the following December. In July, EB and Lota visited Robert Lowell and his wife Elizabeth Hardwick in Castine, Maine. When Lowell began paying EB excessive attention, she and Elizabeth Hardwick agreed to discourage Lowell from venturing alone to Brazil. Elizabeth also went to see Jane Dewey in Maryland and Marjorie Stevens in Key West. In mid-October Lota and EB set off by slow freighter for Rio, bringing with them crates full of American food and household goods on which, to their annoyance, the Brazilian Customs made them pay duty.

They spent Christmas on Cabo Frio with Brazilian friends, returning to Petrópolis in the new year.

1958

Relieved to be home again, Lota threw herself into finishing the Samambaia house. Two of Lota's adoptive grandchildren and a-nephew of fifteen joined the cook's babies in a household that EB found bizarre but entertaining. She was not writing much poetry. The snarls of Brazilian politics, meanwhile, grew weirder as the corrupt [Quadros] Government sought to brighten its image by building a new ultra-modern capital city, Brasilia, in the midst of a jungle accessible only by air. Carlos Lacerda, journalist, populist politician and friend of Lota's, vehemently opposed a policy that left the needy of Rio unprovided for; Lota and EB supported him.

In the summer, the American author John Dos Passos arrived in Rio to write up Brasilia for the *Readers' Digest*. Three or four weeks later, he was followed by Aldous Huxley and his wife. When it transpired that the Huxleys, with a group of foreign journalists, were being flown into Brasilia by the Air Force, EB elected to go with them. With the group, she toured Brasilia and was then flown on to Minas and the Mato Grosso to visit 'unspoiled' tribes of Indians. Reporting to Robert Lowell late in August, EB declared that it was 'the best trip I've made here so far.' She found the Indians naked, friendly, and childlike. One widower, having discovered her to be female despite her trousers, politely asked her to marry him. 'We flew over the River of Souls, the River of the Dead.. to the *Xingu*,' she wrote to Lowell, explaining that she was 'finishing a piece about it' for the *The New Yorker*. The article was rejected but in July 1959, *The New Yorker* was pleased to accept EB's long poem 'The Riverman', written before she had seen the Amazon. 'Brazil, January 1, 1502' was begun soon after this trip, one of a group of poems that, years later, became the first section of *Questions of Travel*.

In October 1958 Robert Lowell sent EB a manuscript copy of

Life Studies – a collection that was to change the direction of American poetry in the 1960s. Bishop was enthusiastic, though in years to come she would have little sympathy with 'confessional poetry'. To Lowell she mentioned that she was thinking of accepting invitations to lecture on American democracy; she was 'reading American poetry with new ideas.' Lowell was by that time teaching at Boston University where Sylvia Plath and Anne Sexton were among his students.

1959

EB sent Lowell a draft blurb for the jacket of *Life Studies*. On July 9, after *The New Yorker* had accepted 'The Riverman', she reported to Anny Baumann, her New York doctor, 'I've been doing a whole group of poems again at last thank heavens.' The group would include 'Questions of Travel', 'Squatter's Children', 'Manuelzinho', 'The Armadillo' and 'Song for the Rainy Season'. But politically and economically, life in Brazil was becoming desperate. Carlos Lacerda moved from Petrópolis to Rio, hoping to build up his power base, and from June to July Lota and EB followed him. They had planned to spend time in New York, December through March, but the drastic inflation of the *cruziero* against the dollar put travel to the United States out of the question.

1960

Disheartened by Brazilian politics, EB arranged in February to travel by boat down the Amazon with a friend of Lota's, Rosalinha Leao, and her young nephew. On February 17, the three flew inland and north to Manaus where the Amazon joins the Rio Negro and there took a boat down river to Belém on the coast. The cruise lasted for three weeks. Santarém (see maps page 162) is located at the junction of the Amazon and the Tapajos Rivers. 'It is much more beautiful than I ever imagined,' EB wrote to Lloyd Frankenberg in March. On April 22, writing to Lowell to congratulate him on *Life Studies* having won the National Book Award, she added, 'I want to go back to the Amazon. I dream dreams every night – I don't know why I found it so affecting.' At the same time she was homesick. 'It is one of my greatest worries now – how to use everything and keep on living here . . . and yet be a New Englander herring-choker bluenoser at the same time.' (One Art, p.383.)

In May 1960 EB and Lota visited the baroque town of Ouro Prêto, where Lota's friend Lilli Correia de Araujo – the Danish widow of a Brazilian painter – ran an inn, famous among Brazilian intellectuals, called the Pouso do Chico Rei. After re-reading Trollope's North America later that summer, EB revised her poem, 'From Trollope's Journals', to send to Lowell. In September, on Lowell's recommendation, she received $7000 from the Chapelbrook Foundation. In the same month, she made yet another expedition by boat to an unspoiled eighteenth century port called Parati. By this time the Brazilian elections were approaching, with Carlos Lacerda running for governor of the new State of Guanabara – which included Rio de Janeiro. When he won in October, he appointed Lota to supervise the building of a people's park on the waterfront. Lota and EB moved permanently to the city, spending weekends only at Samambaia. At first Lota's job delighted them both; to give Rio a people's park was the dream of Lota's life, and she was soon drawing up plans with the best landscape architects in Brazil. EB, however, had suddenly to spend long days by herself.

1961

In June, Time Inc. offered EB $10,000 to write the Life World Library Guide to Brazil. EB decided to accept the offer. Apart from the attractive stipend, the job would pay her way to New York in November/December, when she hoped Lota would be free to join her. As it happened, Carlos Lacerda found it politically expedient to leave Brazil in December. Lota and EB flew to New York that month, borrowing Loren MacIver's empty apartment in Greenwich Village. As might have been anticipated, EB was soon at loggerheads with the editors of the *Time-Life* series, and later she was sorry that she had agreed – for the only time in her life – to write a book for money.

1962

EB and Lota returned to Rio in January, where Lota became busier than ever as a city councillor and official overseer of Flamingo Park. In July, EB welcomed Robert Lowell and his family to Rio. She and Lowell met every morning to swim on Copacabana Beach (good snapshots exist of the two poets wading through the waves), and Lowell and Elizabeth Hardwick both lectured and gave interviews. In August, after Elizabeth Hardwick, with their daughter, Harriet, had embarked for the States, Lowell proceeded alone to Buenos Aires. There he spiralled into a full-scale breakdown and had to be flown back to Boston in a strait jacket. EB, furious with the organiser of Lowell's tour for not anticipating his mania, partly blamed herself.

1963

EB never finished a poem, 'Apartment in Leme', which was to have described the sea along the Copacabana, but that spring she did witness, from her apartment balcony, the shooting of an escaped criminal in the Rio hills, after which she wrote, very quickly, all forty stanzas of her ballad 'The Burglar of Babylon'. To her Aunt Grace in Nova Scotia she wrote of drafting a poem called 'Small Painting' (it became simply) 'Poem' in *Geography III*) and of hoping to finish 'The Moose' (not completed until 1972). As Lota continued to occupy herself with the entangled politics of Flamingo Park, EB anxious about Lowell and feeling neglected herself, began drinking heavily. In September she signed herself into a clinic outside Rio, while Lota, also sick with strain and worry, withdrew briefly to Petrópolis.

1964

On April 1, the political crisis that had long been smouldering in Brazil finally flared up. With the backing of Lacerda and some other state governors, the army ousted President Goulart in a coup that lasted forty-eight hours. Surrounded by Goulart's troops, Lacerda barricaded himself in the Governor's Palace, and for a while Lota was shut up with him, with EB frantically trying to get through to her by telephone. When it became clear that the coup had succeeded, Lacerda, who was no militarist, found himself politically isolated. Circumspectly, he decided to spend some time out of the country. In May, EB and Lota followed his example, using EB's Chapelbrook money to visit Venice and Milan in the spring. Lota, anxious about developments in Rio, went back in June while EB travelled on alone to England, spending pleasant weeks with Kit and Ilse Barker in West Sussex. She also went briefly to Cambridge and London. Before she left England, she made a pilgrimage to Down House in Kent, home of one of her heroes, Charles Darwin.

1965

Back in Rio in August, EB was pleased to learn that she had been appointed the 1964 Fellow of the Academy of American Poets and would receive an award of $5000. Houghton Mifflin decided to mark the occasion by bringing out a paperback edition of the 1955 *Poems*. Houghton Mifflin did not, however, publish EB's third book of poems, *Questions of Travel*, which appeared in November, EB having by then transferred her loyalty to Farrar, Straus and Giroux, the far sighted publishers of *The Diary of Helena Morley* (1957).

Throughout 1965, relations with Lota were strained. Still much involved with her park and oppressed by political infighting, Lota worried that Lacerda was no longer powerful enough to guarantee her financial backing. EB, despairing of ever again living in Petrópolis in the old way, bought and began restoring a beautiful, run down 18th-century house in Ouro Prêto, naming it 'Casa

Mariana' – partly because it lay on the road to a town named Mariana, but mainly in honour of Marianne Moore.

1966

While Lota was battling for her park in Rio and builders in Ouro Prêto were supposedly making 'Casa Mariana' fit to live in, EB – against Lota's wishes – agreed to succeed Theodore Roethke as visiting writer in residence at the University of Washington in Seattle. She flew to Washington after Christmas and taught at the University from January to June, suffering from asthma or from Asian flu most of the time. In Seattle she became a friend and drinking companion of the English poet, Henry Reed, and there, too, she met a young married woman with whom she developed an intimate, dependent relationship. EB returned to Brazil and a jealous, distraught Lota in June. In October she arranged for Lota, who had been relieved of responsibility for her park, to travel with her to Amsterdam and England, but Lota continued to be ill and 'difficult'. Finally she broke down. Cutting their trip short, they were back in Brazil in November, when Lota's doctor sent her to hospital for insulin shock treatment.

1967

In January 1967, a frantic EB admitted herself to a clinic in yet another attempt to stop drinking. Although it looked to EB as if she never would be able to knit up the relationship between herself and Lota, she remained in Brazil; in May she made a trip by sternwheeler down the Rio São Francisco to gather information for a book financed by the Rockefeller Foundation she really *did* want to write on the country. The excursion refreshed her, and by June all seemed well. But by the end of the month she and Lota were at loggerheads again, and in early July EB flew alone to New York, where she again borrowed her friends' empty apartment in Greenwich Village. In September, Lota, disobeying her physician, followed her. Early on the morning after her arrival, Lota swallowed a bottle of sleeping pills and fell into a coma. She was taken to St Vincent's hospital where she lived for a few days. She died on September 25.

Concerned friends, including Robert Lowell and May Swenson, flocked to console EB, but not even Dr Baumann could assuage EB's feelings of horror and guilt. Lota's body was shipped by air to Rio for a funeral EB did not attend, but on November 15, she returned to see to details of Lota's estate. Lota had left the Petrópolis house to Mary Morse and the Rio apartment to EB, but Lota's sister was contesting the will, and many of Lota's friends behaved as if they thought EB was responsible for the suicide. EB likened them to buzzards circling a corpse. She even found herself fighting Mary Morse over paintings and books she had left in Petrópolis. Feeling miserable and betrayed, EB remained with Lota's maid in the Rio apartment until she had sold it. Then she moved her possessions to Casa Mariana – as yet uninhabitable – in Ouro Prêto. On Christmas Eve 1967, she flew out of Brazil to join her young friend R. in San Francisco.

1968

In January, EB moved, with R., into 1559 Pacific Street, San Francisco. R., the mother of an eighteen-month-old boy, was, like all EB's partners, eager to help EB forget her troubles and concentrate on writing. She took charge of decorating and furnishing the apartment and initiated Bishop into the sizzling 'hippy' ambiance of the city. Though EB wrote no new poems in San Francisco she felt younger there; despite the chaotic atmosphere of the '60s, she was relieved to be back in the United States. She put away her nearly finished drafts of 'In the Waiting Room' and 'Going to the Bakery' and turned her attention (more safely) to working on an anthology of modern Brazilian poetry she was translating with Emanuel Brasil. (*An Antholoxy of Twentieth-Century Brazilian Poetry*, published in 1972.)

1969–70

In April, the first *Complete Poems* of EB was published In New York by Farrar, Straus & Giroux; it received the 1969 National Book Award. EB used her prize money to fly back to Brazil in May, imagining that she and R. could live happily together in Ouro Prêto. She had reckoned without the Ouro Pretians' natural mistrust of outsiders and Lilli Araujo's disapproval of EB's new partner. EB lived with R. in Casa Mariana until R. could stand it no longer. After a serious breakdown, which EB seems not to have handled very well, R. and her son returned to Seattle in May 1970. In the summer, Robert Lowell once again came to EB's rescue with a proposal for the autumn. Would EB take over his teaching post at Harvard University while he was away in England? EB, desirous of getting out of Ouro Prêto for a time, gratefully accepted the offer.

1970–71

EB arrived in Cambridge, Massachusetts, on the 24th September 1970. She was given rooms in Kirkland House where, in a dreary basement lecture-room, she was expected to teach two courses for the Creative Writing Program: 'Verse-Writing' and 'Studies in Modern Poetry'. Her duties were not arduous – only two days' teaching a week – but the superior attitude of the Harvard English Department chilled her. As a shy, very private woman, she could scarcely hope to make the kind of impact Lowell did on the students; and the Creative Writing Program was, in any case, academically suspect at Harvard. The playwright William Alfred made her feel as much at home as he could, but EB was again miserably lonely until a young Administrative Assistant at Kirkland house befriended her. For the remaining nine years of EB's life, Alice Methfessel was her indispensable companion.

EB taught at Harvard through January 1971, and was back in Ouro Prêto for her sixtieth birthday in February. Shortly after her return she received news of Lota's nephew Flavio's suicide – only months after his wedding. She was sure Brazilian politics had killed him, just as they had killed Lota. When in April the Brazilian authorities awarded her the Order of Rio Branco for her services to the country, EB was on the point of breaking with Brazil forever. She cancelled her contract with the Rockefeller foundation for a further book on the country and rushed back to New York when she discovered that what she had taken to be alcohol-sickness was in fact typhoid fever. By the end of May she was in a New York hospital being looked after by Dr Baumann. In June, she collapsed in Alice Methfessel's apartment on Chauncy Street, where she stayed for a month, writing 'Five Flights Up' but little else. Once she was well enough to travel, EB was obliged to return to Ouro Prêto; but on August 2 she set off with Alice from Equador for a cruise to Darwin's Galapagos Islands, where they spent 'five wonderful days'. On the way back, they stopped to see the Inca ruins at Manchu Picchu in Peru. The trip restored EB's health almost completely. Back in Cambridge in time for the beginning of the fall term in September, EB settled into an apartment Alice had found her on Brattle Street and finally turned her mind to writing again.

Most of the poems EB had drafted in the 1960s were now ready or almost ready to go public. *The New Yorker* had published 'In The Waiting Room' in July – EB's first finished poem in three years. She also sent *The New Yorker* a 'complete' version of 'Crusoe in England', a poem she had been writing, on and off, since August 1964. But EB was still not ready to deliver herself of 'The Moose'. Teaching at Harvard seemed easier that fall when for the first time she offered a course on poets and their letters. In November, however, she suffered from an asthma attack that put her into hospital for a month. Adrenalin injections and, at one point, an oxygen tent pulled her through. By December she was skiing, bicycling and playing ping-pong, rejoicing in a new set of Harvard friends. Perhaps because The Writing Program was looked down on by conventional Harvard professors, the writers who participated in it became something of a rebellious clique. EB's colleagues included the Mexican poet Octavio Paz, and his wife

Marie Jo, James Merrill, Frank Bidart, Jack Sweeney, Reuben Brower, Albert Lacerda, William Alfred and Helen Vendler, with a fringe that extended up the Massachusetts coast to the Duxbury home of John Malcolm Brinnin. As a group, EB and her friends felt superior to the vastness of popular, mass-produced American poetry, while holding out against professorial 'fogies' and the more pretentious academics.

1972

The year began sadly with the suicide of John Berryman on January 6, followed by the death of Marianne Moore – helplessly bed-ridden – early in February. EB attended Moore's memorial service in New York with her old friends Louise Crane, Margaret Miller and Dr Anny Baumann. In March, Robert Lowell sent EB a manuscript copy of *The Dolphin*. By this time Lowell had left Elizabeth Hardwick and Harriet and was living with Caroline Blackwood in England. *The Dolphin* told the tale of his marital separation and suffering, and to vivify the poems, he had used, and changed, passages from Hardwick's letters. EB was horrified. On 21 March 1972, she wrote back to Lowell, 'One can use one's life as material – one does anyway but these letters – aren't you violating a trust? IF you were given permission – IF you hadn't changed them . . . But *art just isn't worth that much*.' Quoting from Thomas Hardy and Henry James, she held forth passionately about the iniquities of the 'confessional movement' and the temptations it offered writers to exaggerate and even lie about their private experiences. Warning Lowell that by publishing *The Dolphin*, he would wound Hardwick and incur the disgust of the reviewers, EB gave way to feelings that must have troubled her ever since her return to the States: 'I just hate the level we seem to live and think and feel on at present.' (*One Art*, pp.561–2.) Lowell defended himself and published *The Dolphin* in June 1973. As EB had anticipated, the book did wound Elizabeth Hardwick, and Lowell was indeed severely attacked by (especially women) critics.

In June 1972, nearly twenty-six years after she had conceived it, EB finally completed 'The Moose'. She read it at the Commencement ceremony at Harvard – later confessing that it was the only one of her poems her Nova Scotia relatives actually liked. After the ceremony, EB flew to Ouro Prêto to pack her belongings and books; she had decided to sell the last of her three 'loved houses' (the second house in Petrópolis now belonged to Mary Morse) and move to Cambridge. In August, EB and Alice Methfessel cruised to Scandinavia, visiting Stockholm, Helsinki, Leningrad and Bergen, making a side trip on a Norwegian mailboat to the North cape of Norway. On returning to Harvard in September, Bishop was distressed to hear that Lowell would be back teaching in 1973, displacing her, who had only been given the job in his absence. She had arranged to spend the spring term of 1973 at the University of Seattle again, which would pay her enough to take the fall term off at Harvard. But after that? She was relieved when, in March 1973, Harvard offered her a teaching contract, independent of any arrangement with Lowell.

EB's contract with Harvard would begin in the spring of 1974 and end with her 'retirement' in the spring of 1977. To earn money before 1974, she gave readings at Bryn Mawr, Oklahoma, Wellesley, the University of Virginia, and one she enjoyed very much with James Merrill at the YMHA in New York. Working on poems again, Bishop finally completed '12 O'clock News' – a little 'joke' she had begun at Vassar in the 1930s. James Merill, to whom she sent it for comments, replied that he thought it was her 'saddest' poem. In November, *The New Yorker* published 'Poem' – the second of her poems to brood on a painting by her uncle George Hutchinson. (The first was 'Large Bad Picture' published in 1946.) With 'Poem', 'The Moose' and 'Crusoe in England' completed, EB had the substance of her fourth and last collection, *Geography III*, well in hand.

1973

EB taught from March through May at the University of Washington, Seattle, having already arranged to buy an apartment in a warehouse conversion that was going up on Lewis Wharf overlooking Boston Harbour. To Dr Anny Baumann she described her find as being on the 4th floor, with a verandah from which one could watch ships and fishermen, 'high beamed ceilings; exposed bricks, a fireplace' and views such as she had not enjoyed since leaving Brazil. Early in June, EB travelled back to Cambridge from Seattle by way of San Francisco and Palo Alto to spend the rest of the summer in Cambridge writing a memoir of Marianne Moore ('Efforts of Affection'). Weekends were spent on the coast, swimming with John Malcolm Brinnin in Duxbury and with a school friend Rhoda Sheehan, in Westport. It was the summer of the Watergate hearings in Washington; and, for the literary world, of the publication of Lowell's *The Dolphin*.

1974

EB began teaching at Harvard according to her contract, and in April returned to Ouro Prêto, hoping she had sold her house. (The sale fell through.) In May, she gave readings in New York and Washington D.C. and then flew to Washington State to give the annual Theodore Roethke memorial reading in Seattle. Retreating to John Brinnin's Duxbury house in the summer, she worked on a new poem, 'The End of March', which she dedicated to Brinnin and his partner, Bill Read. She had hoped to move into her Lewis Wharf apartment in July, but it was not yet ready, so with Alice Methfessel she rented a farmhouse called Sabine Farm on the island of North Haven, off the coast of Maine. It was an 'island paradise' to which she returned every summer for the rest of her life. By October 1 she had moved into 437 Lewis Wharf, moving in crates of books from Brattle Street while waiting for trunks of more books and possessions to arrive from Ouro Prêto. EB received the Harriet Monroe Poetry Award in that year.

1975
EB received the St Botolph Club (Boston) Arts Award and taught for both terms at Harvard.

1976
The Neustadt International Prize for Literature of $10,000 was awarded to EB on April 9, at a ceremony at the University of Oklahoma. Earlier, however, a crisis in EB's life with Alice Methfessel had brought about a deep depression with a destructive bout of drinking. Writing herself out of a near suicidal state of mind, she produced, after seventeen drafts, her only villanelle, 'One Art'. It was the last poem Bishop finished for *Geography III*, a collection Farrar, Straus and Giroux brought out in December 1976. It won the 1977 Book Critics' Circle Award and unstinted praise from its reviewers. Helen Vendler, in the *Yale Review*, singled out 'Crusoe in England': 'A poet who has written this poem really needs to write nothing else.' Other reviewers remarked on EB's 'radiant patience' and her unromanticised journeys of the mind. (See Millier, p.527.)

1977
At the end of May, EB retired from Harvard University, an internationally famous and personally beloved poet. Ill with an hiatus hernia and anaemia, she went immediately into a Boston hospital and then with Alice retired to North Haven to recuperate. Never prolific, her impulse to write new poems disappeared in the 'hoopla' created by the success of *Geography III*. She worked that summer on 'Santarém', dating from her Amazon adventure of 1960; and on 'Pink Dog' begun in 1963. On September 12, while on a brief return trip to North Haven, she heard from Frank Bidart that Robert Lowell had died of a heart attack in a New York taxi. She rushed back to Boston for the funeral, but had almost immediately to fly to New York to take up a part-time teaching job at New York University. Commuting between Boston and New York for the fall term reactivated her hernia, and she was ill, off and on, until after Christmas.

1978

The worst blizzards in many years hit the East Coast of America in February. EB mainly stayed in Cambridge, writing prose ('Primer Class?') and correcting a proof of 'Santarém', which appeared in *The New Yorker* late in February. In late March, EB learned the she had been awarded a Guggenheim Fellowship of $21,000, to run from September 1978 through September 1979. She planned to write a new book of poems, *Grandmother's Glass Eye*, and a Lowell-like book-length elegy for Lota de Macedo Soares. She never got very far with either of these projects.

In March, after a two-day memorial service for Lowell held at Harvard, Alice Methfessel drove EB to 'Outer Banks', a bird sanctuary in North Carolina, and then on to Arkansas for a week of readings. Honours continued to rain upon her. She was made consultant at Bryn Mawr College for the Marianne Moore Manuscript Collection and in June she received an honorary degree from Princeton. She and Alice then retreated, as usual, to North Haven where they were joined by Kit and Ilse Barker and their son, Thomas. EB appeared relaxed, despite her anaemia, writing 'North Haven' in memory of Robert Lowell and spending days outdoors making notes on flowers and birds. She moved back to Lewis Wharf in the fall for the usual round of readings, honourings and social gatherings.

1979

In May, EB and Alice Methfessel travelled to London where Alice became ill with suspected appendicitis. They visited the Barkers in Sussex and then flew to Venice to take a Swan Hellenic cruise for about a week. EB was not well, but went ashore on the Greek Islands, though she did not climb hills. Back in Boston in September, she signed copies of a broadside (poem-poster) of 'North Haven', for which Kit Barker had provided a drawing. In her last year, EB finished only one new poem, the abbreviated 'Sonnet' which can be seen to sum up her divided life and her hard-won triumph. In Boston, MIT had appointed EB visiting professor of poetry for the fall term of 1979, but she was too ill to take classes. On October 6, Elizabeth Bishop died of an embolism in her home on Lewis Wharf.

Maps

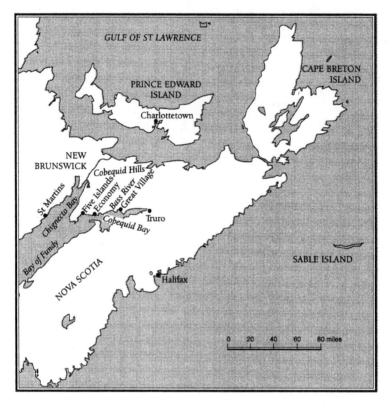

Nova Scotia showing places along the Moose Route from Great Village
to New Brunswick; Sable Island to the south-east.

Brazil. Elizabeth Bishop's home from 1952 to 1967.

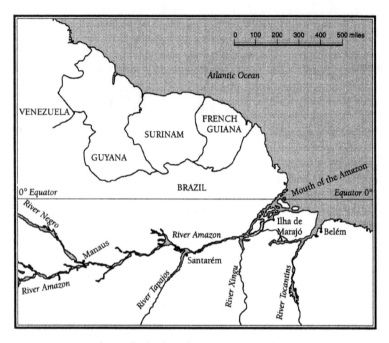

Amazonia where Elizabeth Bishop spent part of 1960 travelling
downstream from Manaus to Belém.

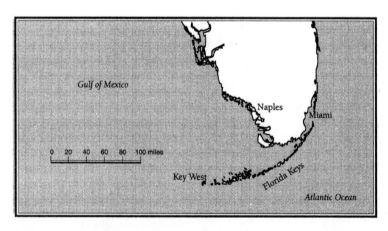

Elizabeth Bishop's Florida, 1936–46.

Notes

Author's Preface

1 Lloyd Schwartz and Sybil P. Estess, eds., *Elizabeth Bishop and Her Art* (Ann Arbor: University of Michigan Press, 1983), p.281.

Chapter One: In the Waiting Room

1 Gary Fountain and Peter Brazeau, eds., *Remembering Elizabeth Bishop: An Oral Biography* (Amherst: Massachusetts University Press, 1994) pp. 152–153. [Henceforth referred to as REB.]

2 EB Notebooks, Vassar College Library; David Kalstone. *Becoming a Poet* (London: Hogarth Press, 1989), p.15.

3 I am grateful to Sandra Barry for information regarding Gertrude Bishop's illness and hospitalisation.

4 EB letter to Anne Stevenson [henceforth AS], 20 March, 1964. Quoted in Kalstone, p.25.

5 See Victoria Harrison. *Elizabeth Bishop's Poetics of Intimacy* (Cambridge: Cambridge University Press, 1993), chapter four. [Henceforth Harrison.]

6 *Ibid.*, p.108.

7 *Ibid.*, p.114.

8 Schwartz and Estess, p.32.

9 Kalstone, p.15; see also the 'Darwin Letter' to AS. 8 January, 1964 quoted in Schwartz and Estess, p.288.

10 Chase Twichell, 'Everything Only Connected by 'And' and 'And': The Skewed Narrative of Elizabeth Bishop' *New England Review and Breadloaf Quarterly*, 8.1, 1985. See Harrison, p.21.

11 Harrison, p.126.

12 *Ibid.*, p.136.

13 Schwartz and Estess, Interview with George Starbuck, p.318.

14 Kalstone, p.21.

Chapter Two: Time's Andromeda

1 Sandra Barry, *Ellizabeth Bishop: An Archival Guide to Her Life in Nova Scotia*, p.193. Published by the Elizabeth Bishop Society of Nova Scotia 1996.

2 Harrison, pp.42–5.

3 EB letter to AS, 8 January 1964.

4 Barbara Swain, letter to AS (Mrs. Anne Elvin), 22 March 1964. (REB, p.40.)

5 REB, pp.42–49.

6 REB, p.40. One of EB's prep-school English teachers wrote of her, when she was found sleeping on the school steps after running away from her aunt's house in Stockbridge: 'Unfortunately she seems to have got the idea in her head that people think her odd and that nobody loves and admires her. *Apparently her longing for affection seeks compensation in the bizarre* [my italics]. Because I believe it very bad for her to think that she is in anyway "odd" or "different" – as such a talented girl is likely to think, I have told her that most people have impulses to run away at times.' (REB, pp. 32–33.) This contrasts with a transparently romantic Christmas note of December 1928 from a favorite English teacher who was evidently much closer to EB. See Robert Giroux. ed., *One Art: The Selected Letters of Elizalieth Bishop* (London: Chatto & Windus, 1994) p.3.

7 EB celebrated the merger with a spirited 'Epithalamium':

> Hymen, Hymen, Hymenaius
> Twice the brains and half the spaeus
> *Con Spirito* and *The Review*
> Think one can live as cheap as two. . .

Literature had reached a deadlock,
Settled now by holy wedlock!
And sterility is fled,
Bless the happy marriage bed. (REB, p.52.)

8 Robert Giroux, ed., *One Art: The Selected Letters of Elizabeth Bishop* (London; Chatto & Windus, 1994) p.9. [Henceforth OA.]
9 *Ibid.*, pp.11–12.
10 *Ibid.*, p.12.
11 Letter of 10 December, 1933, *ibid.*, p.13.
12 'Time's Andromedas' was published in the *Vassar Journal of Undergraduate Studies*, 7 May 1933, pp.102–120. 'Dimensions for a Novel' appeared in the *Vassar Journal of Undergraduate Studies*, 8 May 1934, pp.95–103. Typescripts of these essays are preserved in the archives of the Vassar College Library.
13 REB, p.57.
14 Kalstone, pp.55–56.
15 OA, pp.34–37; REB, pp.364–365.
16 See the interview with Frank Bidart, REB, p.70.
17 REB, pp.44–47, 67–68.
18 REB, pp.68–70.
19 OA, p.54.
20 Interview with Ashley Brown, Schwartz and Estess, p.297. First published in *Shenandoah* 17, no.2 (Winter 1966) pp.3–19.
21 Harrison, p.83.

Chapter Three: Living with the Animals
1 EB unpublished letter to AS, 8 January 1964.
2 From 'As We Like It' (1948) in Schwartz and Estess, p.278.
3 EB letter to Dr Anny Baumann, 24 June 1955, quoted in Brett C. Millier, *Elizabeth Bishop: Life and the Memory of it* (Berkeley, CA: University of California Press, 1993), p.276. [Henceforth Millier.]
4 OA, p.141.

5 EB unpublished letter to AS, 20 March 1963.
6 Millier, p.287.

Chapter Four: The Geographical Mirror
1 REB, p. 63; OA, p.33.
2 OA, p.125–126.
3 EB unpublished letter to AS, 8 January 1964.
4 'new, tender, quick' are the last words in George Herbert's poem 'Love Unknown' on which EB modelled her poem 'The Weed'.
5 Millier, p.182.
6 REB, p.73–74.
7 Kalstone, p.54.
8 OA, p.68.
9 William Benton, ed., *Exchanging Hats: Paintings by Elizabeth Bishop* (New York: Farrar, Straus and Giroux, 1996). Published in Great Britain in 1997 by Carcanet Press Ltd., Manchester M3 5BQ.
10 Robert Giroux, ed. *Collected Prose* (London: Chatto & Windus, 1994) p.33.
11 In a letter to AS of 30 December 1963, Bishop remarked 'I have always been weak at philosophy . . . Like M. Jourdain speaking prose – I must have been philosophising without realizing it.' Earlier that year (March 20), she protested. 'I don't much care for grand all-out effects,' though she confessed to admiring Lowell's poetry, much of which 'couldn't be more all-out.'

Chapter Five: Geography III
1 *New York Times Book Review* (6 December 1981), p.68. Reprinted in Schwartz and Estess, p.267.
2 See the allusions to Wallace Stevens in Harold Bloom's foreword to Schwartz and Estess, *Elizabeth Bishop and her Art*.

Index of Poems and other Works discussed in this Book

Selected Bibligraphy

Books by Elizabeth Bishop

POETRY – in chronological order
North & South. Boston: Houghton Mifflin, 1946.
Poems: North & South – Cold Spring. Boston: Houghton Mifflin, 1955.
Questions of Travel. New York: Farrar, Straus & Giroux, 1965.
Geography III . New York: Farrer, Straus & Giroux, 1976.
Complete Poems. New York: Farrar, Straus & Giroux, 1983. London: Chatto & Windus, The Hogarth Press 1983, pb 1991.

PROSE – in chronological order
The Diary of Helena Morley (Translation). New York: Farrar, Straus & Giroux, 1957.
Brazil (with the editors of Life). Life World Library. New York: Time, 1962.
An Anthology of Twentieth-Century Brazilian Poetry. Edited with Emanuel Brasil, Middletown, Conn.: Wesleyan University Press, 1972.
Collected Prose. Edited, with an introduction by Robert Giroux, London: Chatto & Windus, The Hogarth Press 1984, pb 1994.
One Art: Selected Letters. Edited with an Introduction by Robert Giroux. New York: Farrar, Straus & Giroux, 1994. London: Chatto & Windus, 1994.

171

Book-length Studies of Elizabeth Bishop

(in chronological order)

Stevenson, Anne. *Elizabeth Bishop*. Twayne's United States Authors Series, New York: Twayne, 1966.

Schwartz, Lloyd and Estess, Sybil P., eds. *Elizabeth Bishop and Her Art*. Ann Arbor: Michigan University Press, 1983.

Parker, Robert Dale. *The Unbeliever: The Poetry of Elizabeth Bishop*. Chicago: University of Illinois Press, 1988.

Travisano, Thomas J. *Elizabeth Bishop: Her Artistic Development*. Charlottesville: University Press of Virginia, 1988.

Kalstone, David. *Becoming a Poet: Elizabeth Bishop with Marianne Moore and Robert Lowell*. Ed. Robert Hemenway. New York: Farrar, Strauss & Giroux, 1989; London: The Hogarth Press, 1989.

Costello, Bonnie. *Elizabeth Bishop: Questions of Mastery*. Cambridge, London: Harvard University Press, 1991.

Goldensohn, Lorrie. *Elizabeth Bishop: The Biography of a Poetry*. New York:Columbia University Press, 1992.

Harrison, Victoria. *Elizabeth Bishop's Poetics of Intimacy,* Cambridge, England: Cambridge University Press, 1993.

Millier, Brett. *Elizabeth Bishop: Life and the Memory of It*. Berkeley and Los Angeles: University of California Press, 1993.

Fountain, Gary and Brazeau, Peter, eds. *Remembering Elizabeth Bishop: An Oral Biography*. Amherst: The University of Massachusetts Press, 1994.

Barry, Sandra. *Elizabeth Bishop: An Arachival Guide to Her Life in Nova Scotia*. Halifax N.S: The Elizabeth Bishop Society of Nova Scotia, 1996.

www.ingramcontent.com/pod-product-compliance
Lightning Source LLC
Jackson TN
JSHW011938131224
75386JS00041B/1432